SCHOOLS OF FISH!®

Also from The Creators of The FISH! Philosophy®

A Remarkable Way to Boost Morale and Improve Results

Real-Life Stories to Help You Transform Your Workplace and Your Life

A Remarkable Way to Adapt to Changing Times and Keep Your Work Fresh

A Remarkable Way to Achieve Your Dreams

SCHOOLS OF FiSH!

Welcome Back to the Reason You Became an Educator

by Philip Strand, John Christensen and Andy Halper

ChartHouse International Learning
Burnsville, MN

NEW YORK

Literary development by project editors, Phil Strand and Steve Mintz.
Cover and interior design by ChartHouse International Learning Corp., Burnsville, Minnesota.

Library of Congress Cataloging-in-Publication Data

Strand, Philip.
  Schools of FISH! : welcome back to the reason you became an educator /
by Philip Strand, John Christensen, and Andy Halper.
     p. cm.
  Includes bibliographical references and index.
1. Motivation in education.
2. Classroom environment. I. Christensen, John, 1959- II. Halper,
Andy. III. Title.
  LB1065.S844 2005
  371.1--dc22

                              2005029784

ISBN 1-4013-0300-5

This book and all other ChartHouse materials are available at ChartHouse International Learning Corporation.
221 River Ridge Circle, Burnsville, MN 55337
866.469.2705
www.charthouse.com

First Edition

Dedication

To my mother, Amy, for teaching me the meaning of faithfulness; to my wife, Betsy, for teaching me the meaning of selflessness; and to my daughters, Emma and Sarah, who continually teach me the meaning of joyfulness.

— *Philip Strand*

To my mother, June Christensen, a teacher who opened many hearts, expanded minds, and above all, consistently took time to Be There for young people. Like all outstanding educators, she guided me in remarkable and loving ways.

— *John Christensen*

To *those* teachers—the ones students describe as their favorites. Because no matter what, even in the moments when they secretly wish for the return of corporal punishment, the profession seems manic depressive, and two plus two equals purple, they know that there is nothing more worthwhile or satisfying than being a great teacher.

— *Andy Halper*

Table of Contents

Introduction viii

A TEACHER'S STRUGGLE

Stinky Fish 3

BE THERE

Be There 14

"Nobody Kept the Good Ones at Home" 17

"The Good Keeps Me Going" 21

The Teacher Who Flunked 29

FISH! Thought: Control vs. Commitment 36

"What Memory Would You Like to Erase?" 39

FISH! Thought: Planting Seeds 50

"It Means No One Ever Has to Be Alone" 51

"Good People Are Waiting for You" 61

PLAY

Play 76

"It's My Job to Care" 79

FISH! Thought: Honest Questions 88

"But You're a Girl" 89

"Who'm I Talkin' To?" 91

The Cheerleader and the Football Player 99

FISH! Thought: Creativity Has No Routine 103

The Book Without an Ending 105

"You Gave Us Back Our Child" 109

MAKE THEIR DAY

Make Their Day 116

A Universal Language 119

FISH! Thought: What's Your Focus? 125

"If You Can't Say Something Nice..." 127

The Unreadable Assignment 129

FISH! Thought: Fear Gets An F 136

Turn It Up a Notch 139

FISH! Thought: First, Live It 145

CHOOSE YOUR ATTITUDE

Choose Your Attitude 148

The "Annihilation" Philosophy 151

FISH! Thought: Who Are *You* Being? 161

"I Caught the Baby on the Way Out" 163

FISH! Thought: New Day, New Choices 170

"Give a Little Part of Yourself" 171

The Attitude Board 175

FISH! Thought: The *Real* Self-Esteem 184

A TEACHER'S PURPOSE

"A Place Kids Don't Want To Leave" 187

Thanks and Acknowledgments 201

FISH! For Schools 204

Study Guide and Online FISH! Resources 205

Sources 206

Background Reading 208

About the Authors 210

Welcome Back to the Reason You Became an Educator

Who was the best teacher you ever had?

For me, it was Bruce Golob. His teaching style was the greatest stand-up routine of intelligent optimism ever. We weren't his audience, we were right in there with him, taking on the world and all of life's crazy ironies. He nudged us not just to find meaning in our lives, but also to actually create our lives. Like acoustic learning gone electric, I remember feeling positive-ly phosphorescent being around his teaching! WOW, that felt good!

He pushed us hard, played with us even harder/smarter. And even when we pushed back, two things were clear: He was real ... He cared deeply.

Every school day (weekends and summers too) educators are asked to change the world, like Bruce changed mine. It's exhilarating, scary, seem-ingly impossible—an undeniably idealistic quest. Because we're not just teaching students to learn. We're inspiring them to want to learn. The teachers I know—and I've talked with thousands of them—charge into the fray with passion and purpose. They care, and it hurts when things get in the way. So much seems outside their control: Administrivia, government mandates, unruly students, sometimes even more unruly parents.

At times like these, as we search frantically for a phone booth where we can put on our tights and cape, it helps to remember that each of us already possesses a strength more powerful than a steaming locomotive. We control how we show up for our students and colleagues.

This book is about educators, everyday heroes who choose to show up in a certain way. And they all have something in common: The FISH! Philosophy.

What in the heck is The FISH! Philosophy?

Few people show up quite like the fishmongers of Pike Place Fish in Seattle. Their work is cold and exhausting, yet they bring so much energy, creativity, and poetic surprise to the job that people come from around the world just to watch. Kind of like observing a classroom … team-taught by Billy Crystal, Muhammad Ali, Albert Einstein, and Maya Angelou.

After filming at Pike Place Fish several years ago, ChartHouse Learning analyzed hours and hours of footage to put its collective finger on what made that workplace so engaging. ChartHouse zeroed in on four essential ideas.

- Despite continual distractions, the fishmongers were consistently present for customers and for each other.
- They constantly looked for ways to be creative and have fun while working—and found that they accomplished even more.
- They connected with customers, and people just passing by, for no other reason than to brighten their day.
- No matter what the situation, each fishmonger took responsibility for consciously, actively choosing his attitude.

These behaviors were not written in the fish market's strategic plan, but ChartHouse Learning recognized them as something every one of us can do to be more alive at work, at home, in the world. Mindful that an idea, like a child, needs its own identity to grow and flourish, ChartHouse named the four practices: Be There, Play, Make Their Day, and Choose Your Attitude. And The FISH! Philosophy was born.

The FISH! Philosophy has been introduced to millions of people around the world through a video called FISH! and a book of the same name. It's a positive, common language that gives individuals and organizations a foundation for building vibrant relationships.

FISH! For Schools

As educators brought FISH! to school, they told us, "Hey, this sounds a lot like the research on what works with kids. Except more fun!" They were right: We found tons (well, actually several pounds) of studies on classroom management that validated The FISH! Philosophy. From this research, guided by real-life teachers, we created FISH! For Schools, a combination of curriculum, staff development, and workshops, to help educators build more invigorating, effective classrooms and schools.

As we developed FISH! For Schools, educators told us The FISH! Philosophy gave them a way to connect with students like they'd never connected before. As one boy informed his teacher, "FISH! helps you hear me." They said they were rediscovering the passion that had been buried under demands, cynicism, and distractions. Learning was fun again. This book, Schools of FISH!, is their story.

As you read, you'll find ideas that confirm your best instincts, challenge your thinking, and deepen your understanding of The FISH! Philosophy. But most of all, you'll find stories of people just like you, with students, hopes, dreams, and yes, problems like yours. It's about educators who use The FISH! Philosophy to help them BE the best parts of themselves, to ignite the spark that illuminates minds and hearts for life ... to be that teacher, the one your students remember as the best they ever had.

Welcome back to the reason you became an educator.

—Andy Halper,
Professor of Boredom Prevention, ChartHouse Learning

A TEACHER'S STRUGGLE

Stinky Fish

Teaching always came naturally to Chris Streiff.

"We all try different jobs in life. Some are hard. It's not that you *can't* do them, but they're kind of a struggle. Other jobs just come naturally. That's what teaching always was for me.

"Like when I was a student teacher, I would always get down on one knee to talk to children. My supervisor would ask why I was doing that. 'Well, because they're *short!*'" Chris laughs. "Of course she would explain the psychology of how it put kids more at ease—and I learned all that. *I* just did it because it felt right ... and it worked."

Things worked so well for Chris that for her first seven years of teaching in Rochester, Minnesota, she never used a behavior plan. "Basically, my approach was: You respect me and I respect you. I never had a problem building a classroom community."

But then, she encountered a first grade class at Gage Elementary School that just didn't click. "I don't know if it was the mix of abilities, backgrounds, or personalities, but they were a handful," Chris says. "Some of it was that Rochester was changing. We had more children who came to school with a lot of needs.

"One little girl's family had recently emigrated here. Her mother was trying to raise five kids by herself, learn English, and go to school so she could get a job. Another student moved back and forth between Rochester and Chicago every few weeks. She would tell us stories like, 'The police came to our house last night because there was a big fight,' as if this was no big deal. These kids had so much to deal with, and they brought it with them to school."

The needs didn't stop there. One student with autism regularly threw himself on the floor, kicking and swinging his arms. "He'd hit chairs, kids, whatever was in reach. He was a big boy, and it was terrifying for some kids. We taught everyone about autism and tried to not make a big deal out of it. One of the other teachers said, 'How do you do it, Chris? There's yelling coming from your room all the time.' I said, 'Really?' His meltdowns were so frequent that we kind of got used to it.

"Another student was so impulsive that, when I'd call his name, he'd come to me directly over the table, chairs, or whatever person might be in his way. He'd scream in kids' faces if he was upset. He'd run down the hall, push the older kids, and not give it a thought.

"I understand impulsiveness," Chris says. "The kids are little, they're learning, and it's my job to help them learn the right behavior. What bothered me most, though, was disrespect. Kids were rude and mean to each other. Some would laugh when a classmate gave the wrong answer. They argued over crayons and markers, scribbled on other people's work. They hit. They fought. Some stole food from lockers—sometimes because they were hungry. Every transition took half an hour. We talked about it all the time, but we hadn't been able to develop the sense of community

STINKY FISH!

that's necessary in any class."

As a result, the entire class missed out on learning. "One little boy came to kindergarten already reading chapter books," Chris says. "I needed to keep him challenged. But when you spend all your time focused on getting the dramatic behaviors under control, the kids who are ready to roll suffer. Some of them were shutting down. I couldn't let that happen. In first grade, when you're learning to read and kids laugh at you for whatever reason, that can make or break who you become as a reader."

Gradually, Chris's classroom personality began to harden. "I feel I'm a warm person and I always loved to see the kids have fun learning, but I was furious that these kids thought they were running the show, taking away from other kids' valuable learning time. I told Ann Clark, the principal, and Kevin Ewing, the assistant principal, to expect an influx of students from my class because I wasn't messing around anymore. I started sending kids to the office left and right. I had never done that before."

Desperate, she talked to everyone on staff who might have a solution. For the first time, she tried a behavior plan that involved flipping colored cards with each infraction. "That lasted a week. I felt I was saying, 'Strike one, strike two, strike three,' all day.

"I was becoming way too intense to be a first grade teacher. I was so tired trying to control these children all the time. I trudged through the days. The joy was gone. I went home wiped out, and I didn't enjoy my family life. I felt … defeated. You know what was the most frustrating? I thought, 'I'm *good* at teaching! I was *meant* to do this!' But it wasn't working. If I couldn't do what I was meant to do, what was I there for?"

One day, the pressure proved too much and she had a meltdown in Kevin Ewing's office. "I can't keep doing this if I'm not going to be successful," she told him between sobs. At home she began to look through the classified ads. It was only November.

"I was furious that these kids thought they were running the show."

Changing *our* classroom

At about that time, Chris learned about The FISH! Philosophy. "I was the staff development facilitator at Gage and was thinking of ways to apply FISH! to the staff. But my mind kept going back to the classroom. I realized The FISH! Philosophy was a model for behaviors I was looking for with *students*. There was nothing there that wouldn't work in the classroom."

Chris also recognized that she couldn't do it alone. "I realized it wasn't just *my* classroom. It was *our* classroom. I had to find a way for my students to want to make it a better place."

Stinky Fish

Chris started the process by drawing a large fish skeleton on chart paper. "I said, 'Boys and girls, I feel like I'm crabby all the time. I need your help. There are some things in class that are bugging me. Are there any things that are bugging you?'"

Almost all the children, even the ones causing the most problems, were bothered by something going on in the class. Chris and her students identified the things that were interfering with fun and learning and wrote them on the lines of the fish bones: pushing, shoving, blurting out, stealing, budging in line, not sharing. They quickly filled up three large fish bones.

When the class was done, Chris asked, "How do you think a dead fish smells?" To which the kids replied, "Stinky! Smelly!"

"Do we want a Stinky Fish in our classroom?" Chris urged.

"No!" the kids yelled.

"Do we want these behaviors in *our* classroom?!"

"No!"

Suddenly Chris ripped the sheet off the easel, crumpled it, and threw it in the trash. "I'm not overly dramatic, so the children were a little shocked that I would do that to my hard work—and to theirs," she says. "But I wanted them to see the symbolism of throwing these behaviors away."

Chris didn't really throw the Stinky Fish away. "I put it in a special Stinky Fish Trash Bin, so if the behaviors came out in the future, we could take out the paper and look at it again. Occasionally, we'd grab it to remind students that we had thrown those behaviors out."

Practicing values and beliefs

Having identified behaviors they *didn't* want, Chris used The FISH! Philosophy to start a discussion about what the class *did* want. "We looked up the word 'philosophy' in the dictionary and learned that it is a set of values and beliefs that we all live by.

"Can we throw books in class?"

"I didn't tell them, 'These are my classroom rules and here's how it's going to be.' I talked about how 'this is something I'm learning about and I think it can help us, but I'm not sure. Let me share it with you and let's explore it together.' That captivated them, I think. They thought, 'Hey, she thinks we can help.' It was an *invitation*."

Next, Chris showed the FISH! video to her class. "I told them adults use this, and the kids thought that was cool. They felt grown-up." She smiles. The kids watched one section at a time, and then talked about how each principle might work in our classroom. "When we looked at Play— where the guys are throwing fish in the market—one child asked, 'Can we throw books in class?' 'No,' I answered. 'But what *can* we do that's fun with-out throwing? Singing, dancing, chants ...' We tackled one concept a day so the children had a good overview."

Once they knew what FISH! was about, Chris says, "We all had a framework for what we wanted. We were all speaking the same language. If a student did something that wasn't helpful, I could say, 'Do you think that would Make Their Day?' They understood right away. It got them to thinking about how their actions might affect others instead of just thinking, 'I got caught.'"

The final step was to practice FISH! behaviors. "Kids learn by doing. That's the only way to internalize it. So at various times during the day, during transitions, we'd brainstorm ways we could choose our attitudes or Be There. We didn't just put it on flip chart paper. We figured out how to put it in action.

"I knew FISH! was good for kids when they started bringing up, on their own, concepts that we had discussed. Kids would say, 'Can I make my own Stinky Fish?' So I made a bunch of sheets with Stinky Fish bones and put them out for the class. If something was bothering a student, they'd take one, write it out, and put it on my chair. Then we'd talk about it as a class. It gave kids a way to air their concerns without seeming like they were tattling. It was important for them to know they had some ownership over what was happening."

Coloring attitudes

When Chris asked the first graders what an attitude is, they weren't always able to verbalize it. "So they'd show me a face—mad or happy or sad. From there we'd talk about things like, 'If we come to class in a bad mood, what can we do to turn it around?' I told them I like to journal so I can get my feelings out. Once I'm aware of how I'm feeling, I can think about how to change it. From there we came up with an idea of a daily attitude survey."

At the top of the survey sheet were the words *This morning, I feel ...* Next to that were three faces: happy, neutral, and sad. When students came to class each morning, they'd circle the face that matched their mood at the time. "It helped them think about how they were feeling," Chris notes. "Because they might not have realized they were in a bad mood."

Also on the survey were the words, *I will work toward having this attitude today* ... and a second set of three faces. "They'd color in the attitude they wanted to choose," Chris says. "We learned that we all have unhappy stuff that happens in our lives and it's okay to be upset, but we can't come to school and hurt people with words or hands because we had a bad morning at home."

Sometimes, though, it wasn't always that seamless. To help students who brought bad "stuff" with them to class, Chris created a Chat Chair. "Kids sat in it when they wanted to talk privately. Once I got the other students started on their work, anyone could talk to me and get out what was on their mind," she explains. "It was so important to take the time to deal with these kinds of concerns. As all teachers know, if you try to ignore them, they surely come out in some other behavior."

"We all have unhappy stuff that happens in our lives and it's okay to be upset."

From internal to external

Next, to expand the idea of attitudes, the classroom implemented a Make Their Day plan. Every morning, students selected a Popsicle stick, bearing the name of a classmate, from a can. Students then wrote *how* they were going to make that person's day. "I pointed out that they could make *lots* of people's days, but I wanted them to have a specific plan."

At the end of the day, students looked at their planner and saw how they did. "The main idea was to consciously make the effort," Chris says. "Maybe my plan was to play with Katie, but instead I sat with her at lunch or helped her with math or worked together on a project. We did this activity for about three weeks, and after that it just came naturally."

Chris's students were amazed at how making someone's day made them feel. "I saw the boy who had trouble with his impulses tying an autistic boy's shoes in the lunch room. He was thinking about someone other than himself."

Taking care of each other

Chris's class also often talked about what it meant to Be There for others. "A lot of times we don't take time to teach children what we're looking for," she says. "We discussed how being there means eye contact, not talking while someone else is speaking, turning your body toward me, being with me when I give directions. Once they understood that, a simple, 'Are you with me?' was all I had to say when they got off track."

Be There also means respect for others. "If your friend is saying she doesn't want you to do that, or he doesn't want to play that way, you need to tune into that. The children started listening to what one another really saying. Many of their little spats and issues with sharing went away."

Eventually, students started coming to Chris with books they were reading. "They'd tell me, 'This one has something about Be There or Make Their Day,'" she says. "We started a basket of books whose messages reinforced FISH!, so if we had problems I'd grab a book and I had a discussion tool right there."

Being there was especially important outside the classroom. Chris explains, "A lot of our behavior problems happened on the playground or in the halls when students weren't as closely supervised. My kids were the little ones on the playground. To know that they would look out for each other, to support each other, to include each other, was big. Because of that trust, when they came back into the classroom, they felt more comfortable taking risks in their learning and exploring."

One rainy day during indoor recess, when Chris returned to her classroom, the aide told her two of the kids had bonked heads. "Neither was seriously hurt, but when I got there the class was in two groups, each group comforting one of the kids who had collided; just taking care of each other. That summed up the year for me."

As the kids evolved, others got inspired. Kevin Ewing, Gage's assistant principal, started stopping by to join the students in a goofy

"I had a discussion tool right there."

dance. "Since I'm the one dealing with discipline issues a lot," he says, "it helped the kids to see me as a friend, not just the person they go to when they're in trouble."

Chris adds, "It was important for children to see teachers and administrators having fun. Showing kids that school can be fun—even though it's a struggle at times—that's part of the process. Once kids recognized this, they were willing to embrace challenges even more."

Going with the flow

The more fun her kids had with learning and growing, the more Chris relaxed. "I was able to go with the flow of the kids more, to enjoy their personalities." It was apparent in and outside the classroom. Gage's teachers noticed that the old Chris—happy, relaxed, passionate—had returned. Her colleagues wanted to know: What was happening with her? She hadn't gotten a new class. Why was she so centered? What was she doing?

When she shared her FISH! story, many were interested but not yet ready to try the philosophy themselves. "I had great, fabulous teachers tell me, 'It's one more thing. I cannot think about doing one more thing.' But for me, it wasn't about that. As my kids became a community and worked together, it allowed me to become more of a facilitator instead of having to spend all my time watching them. The kids were able to explore learning on their own and I wasn't always fighting this negative air in the classroom. They were doing their job, which gave me time to do my job. It allowed me to get back to who I was and why I got into teaching."

Changing our classroom

Though some of Chris's students couldn't pronounce "philosophy"— "They said *philopopy*," she says—they all understood it was a model for behavior in the classroom. "They were proud of the culture they created and they talked a lot about how things had changed," Chris says. "It was important for them to see they had the power to take a situation that wasn't good and make it better. And they accomplished that."

By the end of the first quarter, nearly 200 behavior slips were given out in the six grade levels, and half were in first grade alone. "Except in my classroom," Chris says. "Behavior slips dropped way off, like 90 percent. Kids were still challenging, but we got through lessons more quickly—everything just flowed. We had finally figured out we were all in this together.

"I think it's this shared ownership that makes The FISH! Philosophy so effective. It isn't something that you do *to* kids. It's something you do *with* them, as partners."

BE THERE

How does it feel when someone gives you his or her undivided attention? By contrast, what's your reaction when those you are trying to communicate with constantly look over your shoulder, check their watches, or continue to work while you are talking? 🐟 Often we're so wrapped up in our own heads, we forget about other people—the very ones for whom we're not being there. Kids, especially, know when we're present. One teacher refers to this as "being in the game." She says, "Kids can sense it if you're not playing 100 percent—and they'll take advantage of it. But if they know you're in the game, it changes the relationship." 🐟 It may also change how they react to their own mistakes. If your relationship with a student is poor, often the reaction is, "I know you don't care about me, so why should I care?" Conversely, if your relationship with a student is healthy—when you're consistently there for them—they may simply say, "I'm sorry. I messed up. Can you help me?" 🐟 That duality also transfers to adult relationships. As daily pressures compete for our attention, it's amazing how people can seem rude or, equally, how simple gestures stand out. For example, a certain principal never answers his phone when talking with a visitor. "It will ring and the other person will say, 'It's OK if you get that,'" he explains. "I tell them, 'No, you're more important to me right now.'

They're always surprised." Why? Possibly because it's such a powerful statement of respect and commitment.

Oh no ... not that student! Be There also centers around how we think about others. For example, it can be difficult to look past the reputation that some students carry with them from year to year, and easy to get locked into negative comments, made offhandedly or not, by colleagues who have taught them before. Instead of getting to know these students as they are today—or who they might become—we may treat them as they were in the past. The student often responds by thinking, "You've already made up your mind about me, so why should I be different?" The relationship remains stuck in a continuous cycle until someone decides to give today (and the possibilities of tomorrow) a chance.

Awareness, commitment, practice Be There starts with the decision to be physically and mentally present. When you get distracted—as we all do—you simply catch yourself and bring yourself back to now. There's nothing magical or mystical about it. All it takes is awareness, commitment, and practice.

"Nobody Kept the Good Ones at Home"

It began with a call from an upset parent.

"She told me that the night before, three boys had gone to her house, yelling for her son to come out and fight," recalls Dr. Hartzel Jennings. "The boys were sixth-graders at the school where I was principal. The conflict boiled down to a lack of acceptance: Someone had said something to someone else, feelings were hurt, and one group decided not to accept the other."

Hartzel called the four boys to his office. "I have a video I'd like you to watch," he said, and he put FISH! in the VCR. "When it was over, I asked them some simple questions: 'Are you making anyone's day? Did you choose actions that were helpful? Can you really Be There for others by fighting them?'

"I didn't expect any miracles," he says. "By the time the boys left my office, they weren't best friends, but the situation did de-escalate. There were no more instances of the three boys trying to get the other student to fight them. The boys understood they could choose to accept each other and move on with their own lives."

"I have a video I'd like you to watch."

Acceptance, affirmation, and caring

Hartzel recently retired as principal of Theodore Roosevelt Elementary School in Cocoa Beach, Florida. He recalls, "When I first came here, I didn't unpack my belongings for a year. The children at the school were arguing and fighting too much. The community was telling me that kids have changed and things were not like they used to be.

"But I looked around and said 'It looks like the same kids to me.' I checked all the houses. Nobody kept the *good* children at home. We had been given the best they had, and it was time for the staff and I to start turning things around."

Again, the tool was acceptance. "I've been in education more than 40 years and I've seen it all," he says. "The one thing I know works with everyone—children and adults—is acceptance.

"What you and I want right now, more than anything, is to be accepted—at home, at work, at the grocery store. We will do almost anything for acceptance. Lack of acceptance is why schools lose kids, why parents lose kids. We say, 'I love you, *but ...*' This kind of love is conditional. Once someone knows, *really knows*, you will accept them—not just when they do things perfectly, but when you show through your words and actions that you care about them—they will do anything for you."

Acceptance shows up in simple ways, Hartzel says. "It's helping children in the lunch line when they're out of money, making time to be with them while they're waiting for the bus, and not thinking something else is more important. It's respect in its simplest form. If there's a line of students in front of me, I don't just cut through them. I open doors for teachers *and* students."

He continues, "I've always asked students to practice the same kind of commitment I have to them. If you're a sixth grader in my building, you're expected to take care of everybody younger than you. It's your job to show them respect and to help them learn. The same is true of every other

"Acceptance shows up in simple ways."

grade, on down the line. The second graders are expected to take care of the first graders, and so on. The only people exempt are the kindergarteners and autistic kids. They're perfect in every way. The rest of us have to take care of somebody."

Acceptance also means remembering that some days, students have more to worry about than reading and writing. "Forty percent of the students at Roosevelt have parents in the military," he says. "Some of them are in harm's way. So we have to watch for kids that need the most attention. We can't tell them it's over and we can't guarantee that Mom or Dad's coming home safe. But we can make a commitment in our hearts to fill that gap with whatever they need from us."

One day, Hartzel asked a student if she had been working hard.

"I sure have," she answered.

"What are you working hard at?"

"I work hard praying that my mom comes back alive from Iraq," she said.

Saving time, teaching responsibility

Hartzel has always had high expectations of himself, his staff, and students. "One mother wanted me to be more understanding of her child's lack of effort," he says. "To her surprise, I responded, 'I won't accept it and *we're* not going to let him accept it. We're going to help him to put 26 letters in the right order so that he can spell. Your job is to go home and support your son. My job is to care for him and to tell him what a wonderful mom and dad he has.'

"It's easy to expect great things from students when they know what to expect from you," he adds. "They have the right to know that I'm not going to give up on them, even when they fall short of their potential. My message to the students is that they may be here in the office because we have a problem, but it's not that I don't accept them anymore. It's another chance to learn."

The FISH! Philosophy is a natural tool for such situations, Hartzel says. "The first group I used it with, even before I used it with the boys who were fighting, was a group of gifted students. Wonderful kids, but they were always arguing. So I invited them to my office and said, 'I'm a happy man today. But I'm also a busy man, so I'd like you to watch this video.'"

Hartzel left the room and peeked through the window. The students looked back at him like he was crazy, but the video quickly grabbed their interest. When it was done, one of the students got up and turned off the TV. Hartzel returned to the room and went to his computer as though nothing was going on. "Oh," he said. "You're still here. So what did you learn?"

"We were all on different tracks," a student responded. "Because we weren't being there for each other, we couldn't get along, and we couldn't get our work done."

"Interesting," Hartzel said. "What are you going to do about it?"

"Well, it's our choice," the kids said. "We choose to be happy *or* upset. If we choose to be happy, we can handle it."

"Sounds good to me. Now, back to class."

"When I followed up with the kids later," he recalls, "they still got the point of the video. We had a fairly high-level discussion about our purpose, and I didn't see any of them in my office the rest of the year.

"I could relate The FISH! Philosophy to just about any situation, and the kids learned and had fun with it. It fit with everything we were trying to do. It said it better than I could. And," he says with a chuckle, "it saved me a lot of work."

"The Good Keeps Me Going"

Several years ago, Bonita Alston was driving a school bus while taking college psychology classes. "One day a boy mistakenly got on my bus," she says. "I asked him his first name and he told me. I asked his last name but I couldn't understand him, so I asked him to spell it. He couldn't—and he was in the third grade.

"I said, 'Why can't you spell your name? You need to know it.' He said, 'That's not what my teacher told me. She said we only have to write our *first* name.'

"I found the bus he was supposed to be on and he saw his sister. I asked her, 'What's your last name?' She said, 'Freeman.' I told her to work with her brother at home. I said, 'He needs to know his first name, last name, street address, and telephone number. Someone told him his last name is not important but it's not true. Your name is who you are. It's important—and *you* are important.'

"The next day I went to the college and told my dean I was changing my major to education. I was going to become a teacher."

"Your name is who you are. It's important—and *you* are important!"

Making it work

Growing up, Bonita often had to Be There for herself. Her father died when she was six and her mother became an alcoholic. "He had abused her and afterward she fell into drinking," Bonita says. "She always had dinner ready for us when we came home. We had to be respectful and we never went to school dirty. No parent wakes up each morning saying, 'Today, I'm going to drink till I can't stop.' But she had a disease."

When Bonita was 13, her mother died. "My older sister got out of the military; we had a house and all of us raised each other," she says. "I took care of two younger siblings. Plus my older sister had a child of her own.

"My sister kept saying, 'I can't do this by myself. You're going to have to go to the orphanage or a foster home.' Instead, I made sure dinner was ready when she came home from work. I helped my younger siblings with their homework. I did the laundry and shopped for groceries. I wanted her to know it could work."

All grown up

After high school, Bonita started college, but soon she met her husband, got married, and had a daughter. He worked in a shipyard while Bonita worked three jobs—at a hair salon, cleaning an office building, and driving a school bus. She says, "I didn't want to do that for the rest of my life. So I went back to school."

Bonita kept her bus-driving job and focused the rest of her time— literally—on school. "I'd make my runs in the morning," she recalls, "go to Norfolk State, finish my bus runs in the afternoon, then go back and take evening classes."

This focus carried over to her 72-passenger bus. "I made four runs a day and I knew every child's name. It wasn't 'Hey, you! Sit down back there!' I knew *every name*. They were my babies. Some days I'd take treats on the bus. I had a contest where they guessed how many jellybeans were in a jar, and the winner kept the jellybeans. I laughed with them and joked with them. I tried to be myself—tried to do little things to make us feel like family."

She also did a lot of listening. "They told me so many things. 'Mrs. Alston, my mother didn't come home last night.' Or 'I'm glad I'm going to school today, Mrs. Alston, we don't have anything to eat at home.' One student told me, 'My mom's selling drugs. The police are watching my house.' I didn't have all the issues as a child that they had, but I did have an unsettled home life. I could relate to their worries."

While a good listener, Bonita also knew when to draw the line. When there were problems, she explains, she wasn't afraid to pull the bus in front of a student's home and talk to a parent. "The kids all knew I'd do it," she says. "I talked to the principal and she said it was okay. I told her, 'If I just write them up and send them to the office, they're not in class. If they're not in class, they're not learning.' My job is to get them there so they can learn."

"I made four runs a day and knew every child's name."

Work hard, play hard

As Bonita worked to become a teacher, she marveled at the support around her. Fellow bus drivers covered for her when her work schedule conflicted with classes. Teachers came forth with encouragement and resources.

"I couldn't have completed my degree without them," she says. "Teachers would come on the bus and tell me, 'Keep going, we're proud of you.' We'd talk about projects I was doing and they'd say, 'Stop by my class-room, I've got some materials you need.' So many people were there for me."

The support paid off. Bonita finished her course work and, today, teaches fourth grade at Merrimack Elementary School in Hampton, Virginia. "My first year," she recalls, "a boy in my class misbehaved. On his own, without me telling him to do it, he apologized to the principal. I thought, 'This is a great school.'

"At Merrimack, our motto is work hard and play hard. I'm the pitcher when we play kickball; I give kids special invitations to have lunch with me; I let the kids suggest new ways of doing things. A student will say, 'At my old school we used to do this activity to get ready for spelling.' So I suggest, 'Okay, get up there and show us how to do it.' Or, I can't sing a lick, so if they're not paying attention, I say, 'If you guys keep on, I'm gonna *sing* the lesson.' Works every time." She grins.

"If you guys keep on, I'm gonna *sing* the lesson."

Facing challenges

Many of Merrimack's students qualify for free or reduced lunch. About 25 percent are children of military personnel. The students perform well on state tests, and Merrimack has been named a Title I Distinguished School. Still, the challenges don't go away just because the teachers and students work hard.

"We have our problems." Bonita sighs. "Sometimes we find condoms and wine and beer bottles on the playground. Drive through the neighborhood and you see people getting evicted. Some of my students, neither parent is working. Or Mom is taking care of her children *and* her sister's kids in the same house.

"Some of my colleagues don't always know what it's like to go through that, and how that can affect a child, but I have an idea. That's the best thing about teaching—trying to reach these students and understand what they're going through."

Still, Bonita admits it's easy to get sidetracked. "You start jumping from one student to another and another, trying to get to meet all the students' needs at once, and in the end you haven't fully been there for any of them. The FISH! Philosophy helped me realize that. Now I'm working hard to really Be There for every student."

Bonita doesn't consider herself the best disciplinarian, but her approach seems suspiciously like Be There. "My discipline is when you don't know how to stand in line, you come over and hold my hand," she says. "I don't know if that's discipline or not, but they like it.

"I talk to them about when I was a little girl. I can't tell them everything that happened to me, but I *will* say, 'When I was in school, I didn't do this or that, and I regret it.' You can see their eyes light up, like 'I'm not gonna let that happen to me!'"

Bonita continues, "I just talk to them. 'You didn't make a wise decision. What should you have done, what could you have done, and what are you going to do next time?' I don't reach them all. If a student has a horrible attitude, I can't get mad or force her to change it. I can show I care, try to help, be encouraging: 'Hey, I know you know how to do this. You had some great ideas yesterday. Can you get those ideas on paper for me?' She might go for it and she might not. But it's her choice."

Finding something to keep

While the challenges are tough, Bonita notes, "It's hard *not* to have a great attitude at Merrimack, because we won't let you. As soon as I hit the school parking lot, I better be ready. Some of these children go through enough that they don't need a grumpy old teacher meeting them in the morning. They don't need me bringing my junk in here."

To gear up for her day, Bonita continues, "I greet the children lined up outside. I go all the way through the building, from one end to the other, saying good morning to everybody till I get to my class. I love to greet people in the morning. I need that."

Bonita also chooses her attitude by thinking about her mother. "My older sister used to say to me, 'How can you be so happy? Don't you know what we've been through?' But I remember how my mother took us to the beach and how much fun we had. I remember my little sister's friend who came over every morning. Even though my mother's fingers were arthritic, she would comb this girl's hair every morning.

"So I'd remember those good things. The *good* is what keeps me going. I think about where I came from, where I didn't want to be, and that fuels me. When I think about my mother, I try to think about the positives. I pulled things from that—things I've wanted to keep in my life. That's my choice."

If you choose to be happy, people around you will be happy, and then people around them will be happy, so it creates a ripple effect. You're affecting more than just yourself.

—Austin, *sophomore*

The Teacher Who Flunked

Every year Julie Howard tells her sixth grade class about a student who failed.

"This young woman went to college, didn't study very hard, was too focused on other things, and flunked out after three semesters," Julie explains. "She worked for three years, got serious about her goals in life, went back to school, applied herself, and became a teacher. At the end of the story I tell my kids, 'Every one of you knows this person.' Eventually, somebody figures out that it's me.

"When I tell them that story, they understand why I'm so adamant that they do their best and stay focused. They also understand I'm not perfect. I tell them they're going to make mistakes during the year and that's OK because 'an error does not become a mistake until you refuse to learn from it.' They're not worried that, 'If I mess up, she's going to hate me' or 'I'm in big trouble.' Once you take away the fear, they are much more willing to take some chances with their learning. It creates a better culture."

"A young woman went to college and flunked out after three semesters."

The plan

It was this classroom culture that was on Julie's mind as she prepared for her second year of teaching at Avon Intermediate School in Avon, Indiana, an Indianapolis suburb. "When our principal showed the *FISH!* video to the staff, I thought, 'This is the avenue to help establish the culture I wanted,'" she says. "The first year I taught I was all about respect and focus and feeling safe, but I didn't have a language or cues to start that conversation with the kids."

Though Julie was focused on preparing her students to take Indiana state tests just four weeks after school started, she made time to show her students *FISH!* and talk about their goals for the year. "The kids agreed they were here to get the best education possible so they could be successful in life," she says. "With so many different personalities, the issue was: What behaviors will help us do that?"

The class started with Be There. "The kids divided into small groups," Julie says. "They talked about 'How can you stay focused from moment to moment? How can you Be There for your teachers? How can you Be There for your friends?' Then they generated lists of ideas to work on for the year.

"The class researched the dictionary for words that reminded us of attitudes we wanted in our class and those we'd like to eliminate. We'd analyze our reading by asking things like, 'What effect would it have made on the plot if a character made a better choice?' It was a way of integrating values into our curriculum and learning standards."

Telling tales

Julie also shared personal stories to jump-start conversations about FISH! principles like Be There. "We talked about how just one inconsiderate thing you do to someone may stick with them the rest of their life. On the other hand, one small thing to make someone's day may stay with them too.

"I told them about a boy who moved into my neighborhood. I was a freshman and he was a sixth grader—the same age as my students. I was president of the student council and when I'd see him in school, I'd say, 'Hey, there's my neighbor!' No big deal. When I went to high school, I'd wave to him on the bus—again, no big effort.

"Several years later, I'm working and I get a phone call: 'Is this Julie Howard?' 'Oh no,' I'm thinking, 'what did I do?' Well, it turned out to be my neighbor boy. We chatted for a while and he said, 'I was in a training session at work, and they asked us to think of a person who had been influential in our lives. I thought of you. It was tough being the new kid but, because you knew me and the younger kids looked up to you, everybody wanted to be my friend.'

"I really didn't do anything," Julie says. "All I did was say 'hi' and smile. So you never know what makes a difference to someone else. My students could relate to my story because it was personal."

Julie continued with another story to show how she emphasized being there. "There are teachers who send a clear message that they don't like certain students. I had a high school teacher who flat out said to me, 'Why aren't you more like your sister? She was so nice and never caused trouble like you.' After that day I shut down and went from an A average to a C in his class.

"When my kids hear that story, they see I can identify with them. I wanted that teacher to care about me—and he didn't. Now that I'm a teacher, I want those kids to know I care about *them*. If they don't get a lesson, I'll figure out a way to help them get it. I care about their choices and actions—not because it helps me have a compliant class—because I don't want them to sell themselves short."

This effort is clear to her students. "One day, some of the kids were saying, 'My friends never have to talk about how they treat each other like

"Why aren't you more like your sister?"

our class does.' I asked, 'Why is that?' A boy raised his hand—and you never know what's going to escape from his lips—and said, 'Well, some teachers just want us to turn in homework and get good grades, but I think you must care about us.'"

The power of reflection

This focus came early for Julie. "One of the best lessons I ever got came when I was a student teacher. My supervisor said, 'When a student gets in trouble, instead of getting frustrated, find out what's *causing* the frustrating behavior.'

"I had a rebellious student with that middle school attitude of 'It's not cool to do well in school.' I tried some things to connect with him and they didn't work. But I didn't give in. And, as I thought it through, it boiled down to the fact that he didn't have the basic skills he needed in sixth grade. He'd rather have people thinking he was bad or misbehaving than thinking he was stupid.

"How do you know that? You're a teacher, not a kid."

"I told him that when I got in trouble as a kid, it was usually because I didn't understand the lesson or wasn't sure what the teacher wanted me to do. Instead of being called on and not knowing the answers, I'd act out so I'd get sent out of the room. He looked at me like, *'How do you know that? You're a teacher, not a kid.'*

"So we made a deal. 'If you don't understand something, let me know. You can do it quietly or however you want, but I'll find time to help you because you need these skills.' Once he knew I cared enough to get to the bottom of the problem—instead of just saying go to the office or here's a detention—he started to choose an attitude that would help him succeed."

This new skill transferred to the student's other choices too. Julie explains, "He was in a group of five boys that repeatedly lost points for not having their materials ready or for discipline problems. One day this boy said, 'Ms. Howard, I want to vote myself off.' Say what? He said, 'I want to vote myself off the group. I can't get my work done.' Several girls asked him to join their group and of course he wanted to join.

"At first, the other boys were a little miffed he had left, but over the next two or three weeks, they started to tell me, one by one, 'This isn't working. We don't make good choices when we're by each other.' Instead of me saying, 'You can't sit here,' they recognized the problem and took responsibility for themselves."

Practice makes perfect

"To me, everything in life is a reflective process. If something's not working, we need to recognize it and change—not just keep doing the same thing over and over. That's what my class did. They realized they are just as important as I am in creating the classroom we want. It gave them a sense of power they hadn't had before."

Julie discusses how the language of FISH! helped make this change. "The FISH! Philosophy helped us to regularly reflect on who we wanted to be. It gave us specific names and cues to the behaviors that would help us get there. Instead of me saying, 'Hold the door open,' or 'Pick up after yourself,' the students took Be There and Make Their Day and figured out to do those things on their own.

"It's essential that students be given the chance to make those choices," Julie says. "I tell kids, 'Do you think you just turn 18 and the clouds part and suddenly you are an all-knowing adult? No, you have to practice, and practice making good choices because if you don't do it now, you won't make good choices as an adult.'"

Can we do it? Yes, we can!

As Julie's classroom became a more reflective place, it also became a safer place. There were fewer put-downs and more encouragement. They caught themselves more quickly when they were off track. When they worked to Be There, Make Their Day, and Choose Your Attitude, the classroom naturally became a more lighthearted place.

"I don't remember how it started but when I'd give instructions, I'd say 'Can we do it?' The students would respond 'Yes, we can!' That's from *Bob the Builder,*™ which is a show that almost every student had watched when they were little.

"It was a joke and totally tongue-in-cheek—kind of like asking sixth graders to sing the *Barney*™ song. But they loved it. I think the kids were saying 'We're part of something.' When we said it, it meant that everyone was ready to go and it was our cue to be ready.

"Students are so concerned about being dorky …"

"At this age," she pauses, "students are so concerned about being considered dorky or not doing things that little kids do. I think the fact that we had adult conversations made it okay to Play. We didn't care what others thought. We just thought it was fun."

This way to Play, however, presented an interesting angle when Julie learned that what's fun to one class is not necessarily fun to another: "That first year, my kids loved stuff like *Bob the Builder*. The next year, the class was like, 'We're too cool for this.' At first, I struggled with that. How could they possibly not like what we had so much fun with the year before?

"I finally realized that when you invite kids to help create your classroom environment, it might not be the same way each year. I couldn't say, 'This is how we Play.' I couldn't force it. I needed to choose my attitude and go with what *they* came up with. FISH! isn't about what I want. It's about what works best for them."

Making progress

As the year went on, one of Julie's students continued to bounce off the walls, but often took forever to do certain tasks. "One day as the kids were changing classes he was fussing around and I was saying, 'Come on, you have to get to social studies.'"

"I'm hurrying, I'm hurrying," the boy said.

"Well, you need to go *faster*."

The boy shot Julie a mischievous smile. "You're lucky," he said. "At the beginning of the year I couldn't even remember what books to take with me!"

Julie paused, then nodded. "You're right. I forgot how much progress you've made. I'm really proud of you. Now pro*gress* yourself to social studies!" The boy grinned and took off.

"At that moment, I realized I need to remember to celebrate my students' accomplishments. Now I always tell them at the end of the year, 'You may not always be in classrooms quite like the one you created here, but now you can use The FISH! Philosophy to reflect on what you're doing to be happy and successful.'"

Julie smiles as she remembers how FISH! made such an impact. "The last day with kids is always so tough. I remember the first year I used FISH!, several of the students were crying. They said, 'Can't you *please* homeschool us next year?!' I told them, 'I don't think they'd let me homeschool 27 kids!' They said, 'No, really! We can do it at Mollie's house! Because she has a really big house!'"

"I don't think they'd let me homeschool 27 kids!"

35

 **THOUGHT**

CONTROL VS. COMMITMENT

In 1977, psychologist Carl Rogers described the traditional classroom: "The teachers are the possessors of knowledge, the students the expected recipients; the teachers are the possessors of power, the students the ones who obey."

We adults spend a lot of time in school teaching students about the strengths of democracy: freedom, choice, and responsibility. We tend to spend less time providing them opportunities to actually practice those skills—the same skills they need to become successful citizens and parents. As the poet John Keats noted, "Nothing ever becomes real until it is experienced."

"It seems to be an 'oxymoron,' " note researchers Mary McCaslin and Thomas L. Good note, "a curriculum that urges problem-solving and critical thinking and a management system that requires compliance and narrow obedience."

This strategy of showing students "who's boss" often forces them to choose between being robots or rebels. Some kids withdraw from academic participation altogether. Others negotiate a live-and-let-live relationship where they agree not to disrupt the classroom as long as they are left alone. Even high achievers sometimes join in text-burning parties at the end of the year or use words like "escape" to describe their feelings about school.

Many educators continue to push control because it was the way *they* were taught.

When pressed, however, these same teachers admit that this approach is as unsatisfying as when they were students. It is no more fun to *control* than to *be controlled*.

Breaking the chain

So how much control should a teacher give students? One way to start is to ask yourself, as noted author Alfie Kohn suggests, "What do you want your students to be like, long after they've left you?" Most of us would say caring, responsible, independent, and creative—not docile, compliant, and unquestioning.

It's helpful to think about *roles*, not just *rules*. Some teachers use The FISH! Philosophy to spark discussion about what each member of the classroom wants the culture to be, and the role each plays in creating such a place. These discussions are the basis of a social contract in which each person is accountable to everyone else for his or her behavior. As teacher Jason Pelowski says, "It's not *my* control. It's not *their* control. It's *our* control." In this environment, the FISH! principles are important life skills to work *on*, not rules to work *against*.

It's often as frightening for students to accept control for their part in the class-room as it is for teachers to give them the opportunity. Having been given little practice in making such choices, they don't always know how to respond. But students don't have to become totally independent overnight; we can help them learn gradually, as with math or any other subject.

There is the chance that, given the choice, kids will at times select the opposite response of the one we want. More often than not, however, with accountability, patience, and respect, chances are kids will arrive at the same place we'd like them to be. And when they get there, they'll be even more committed to their choice because *they* made it, even if the path wasn't always a straight line.

There may be times, Kohn admits, when teachers need students to just do what they say—period. But, he comments, students are more "apt to trust … and go along if blind obedience is the exception rather than the rule."

"What Memory Would You Like to Erase?"

It was 1978, and Dr. Charla Waxman was thinking of ways to keep kids out of trouble.

"I had just taken a job with a drug and alcohol prevention program in Hammond, Indiana, near Chicago. Pretty tough part of town," she says. "To say I was naïve would be an understatement. I thought the way to attract kids was with balloons and face painting. Well, the kids showed up all right, and I did a lot of face painting. What I didn't know was they were asking me to paint gang symbols."

Dr. Waxman has learned a lot about gangs over the past 27 years. Through Chicago-area police departments, probation offices, correctional facilities, and schools, she works with young people who have already committed felonies or whose aggressive behavior may be leading them down that path. Their ages range from six to their early twenties. Many are from the inner city, but a growing number are from the suburbs, and even rural areas.

Hurt secrets

Why do kids join gangs? "They're looking for the same things we all want," Waxman says. "A sense of belonging, acceptance, a family they don't have elsewhere."

According to Waxman, most gang members also carry what she calls a "hurt" secret. "To get to that secret, I ask kids, 'What memory would you like to erase?'" she says. "I asked a 17-year-old, inner city, feared gang-banger. He pulls his knees to his chest, puts his head down and says, 'I'm 11 years old.' This kid's face is red, he's shaking, he's speaking in the present tense like this is right now. And he says, 'I'm on my dad's back. I'm pulling his hair, his coat, his ears, anything I can to stop him from burning my mom's face on the stove again.'

"Months later, I posed the same question to a suburban kid. His parents were both professionals who lived in a $2.5 million house, and he'd been in a gang for a year. 'What memory would you like to erase?' 'My eighth grade band concert,' he says. My first reaction, remembering the other kid trying to save his mother, was like, 'Buck up, buddy.' But I asked him to explain. It turned out he wanted to play soccer and his mother said, 'No. You are going to be in band, you *will* excel, you *will* get a college scholarship, and you *will* be wealthy.'

The kid says, 'By eighth grade, I was the best. I had trophies, ribbons, medals. But at my final eighth grade concert, I had just done a solo and people were applauding. For some reason I scanned the audience and at that moment it sunk in that, not only was my mother not at my concert, she had *never* been to one.'

"Here are totally different kids, totally different situations," Waxman says, "but they both lacked the relationship they wanted. They both had pain and they ran to the same organization."

"This kid's face is red, he's shaking ... And he says ..."

New behaviors, new power

Based on her years of experience, Waxman says, no gang member tries to fail. "Even the worst kids don't walk into school thinking, 'I'm going to be the biggest jerk ever this year and I hope everybody hates me.' Somewhere along the way they get frustrated or hurt. Those things outweigh their ability to cope and they fall apart."

Waxman points out she's never told a gang member he or she must leave the gang. Nor has she ever said the gang is bad. "The gang is a mirror of who they are," she says. "If I break that mirror, they won't respect me because I'm trying to take away the only thing they have available to them at the moment.

"Gangs create many addictions—drugs, alcohol, sex, revenge, guns, thrills, crime. These things may be unhealthy, but they are tangible and the only power these kids know," Waxman says. "My task is to help them become aware that there is an *intangible* power that will help them deal with their pain."

Waxman believes The FISH! Philosophy can connect them to that kind of power. "It offers kids the power to enjoy their lives, to Be There for what's going on around them, to reach out to others, to make real choices for themselves. Whenever I get a new group, we start out with FISH! I challenge them to try one of the four principles during the school day and report back on how it worked … and how they felt."

According to Waxman, Be There is essential, especially for kids who are trying to reconnect with adults they once spurned. "I tell kids there are several things you can do to build relationships with teachers. If you make a mistake, say you're sorry. Ask what you can do to fix it, what they would like you to change. Ask adults for advice; when you do, you are telling them that they matter to you. When you ask an adult for advice, they will fall all over themselves to give it to you. And if you really listen, try what they say; if it works, go back and thank them.

"There is an intangible power…"

"I teach kids to get personal. You're less likely to hurt people you know well and who know you well. The more they know about you, the less likely they'll treat you as an object. If you see a picture on a teacher's desk, ask about it. Be willing to tell them things about yourself. If you make a mistake, the punishment is more likely to be based on what's in your relationship rather than, 'I don't know you, so I don't care how I punish you.'"

As a realist, Waxman also prepares kids for temporary setbacks. "I tell them, 'With some teachers, if you've messed up over and over and all of a sudden you say I'm sorry, it's not going to be good enough for them. Even if you're trying to change, you will sometimes get those responses. That's when you really need to Choose Your Attitude.'"

Altering perceptions

To make healthier choices, Waxman teaches, gang members must become more aware of their surroundings. "Part of being there is paying attention, not falling prey to what's being offered to you but looking a little deeper. People don't offer you drugs because they like you," she says. "For these kids, learning to Be There, to be alert and aware of other peoples' motives, and if it's best for them, will save them."

Awareness of the words they use is also important. "Every gang has a common language that pulls the group together," Waxman notes. "That's why one of my rules is that nobody swears in my groups. To me, swearing is the lowest form of violence. It indicates a lack of control. Choose Your Attitude means *you* are in control of your actions—including the words you use. FISH! gives us a positive language to turn to. It starts to influence the way we think."

Sometimes, however, helping gang members become aware of destructive self-talk requires creative responses. Waxman once worked with a boy who would come to school every Monday with a list of people he was going to beat up. She'd ask why, and his reason would be something like, "Because he looked at me wrong," or "I didn't like his tone."

"One morning as I was talking to this kid," Waxman explains, "I get a phone call. Midway through the call I had an idea … When I hung up, I gave the kid an angry look. He looked puzzled. 'What's the matter?' he asked.

"I said, 'That was Miss _____. I'm sick and tired of the way she talks to me. I think she wants me to kick her butt.' Suddenly he gets a panicked look on his face. I stand up and say, 'Let's go. I'm going to her office to kick her butt.' As we're walking down the hallway, he's saying all the things I had been saying to him: 'You're going to get kicked out of here! This isn't important! She might just be having a bad day!'

"And as he's grabbing me by the elbow to try to stop me, I say all the things he's said to *me* a million times: 'I don't care if I get kicked out! I don't care what happens to me!'

"Finally we get to the teacher's door. I turn around and say, 'What am I talking about?' He stands there for the longest time. 'Is that me?' he says. I nod. 'So you're not going to beat up Miss_____?' I shook my head. I never got another Monday list from him again.

"Now that was unorthodox. It was a risk. I could have been fired for threatening to beat up a teacher in front of a student. But sometimes these kids can't see themselves until you're willing to play with their perceptions a bit."

> "I think she wants me to kick her butt."

Did you forget something?

According to Waxman, students who use drugs and alcohol, who choose violent lifestyles, have lost what it means to be a kid. "If we don't give them that opportunity, they may never see it again. So we play board games, we draw. Sometimes I get out coloring books and they're like, 'Are you nuts?' I'll say, 'Just try it.' The next thing you know, they're having a ball."

Waxman also uses Play to ignite serious discussions. "I often tell kids that with me a game is never just a game. So I'll have them build a structure with Lego® building blocks that describes their life, or their best day, or a person they admire most. They get into it, then we talk about it."

Waxman also finds ways to help the students practice making each other's day. "When a kid does something nice for someone in group, or is really showing progress, they get to keep Pete, our stuffed fish, for a week. Then they award the fish to someone they saw do something cool. I'm careful, though," she adds. "When giving out too many tangible rewards, it's too much of a parallel with what happens in the gang. Pete's great because he's a reminder of the philosophy."

If Waxman has any doubts about the power of Make Their Day, she can point to the result of an impromptu experiment. "I was working with several gang members, 17 to 24 years old, pretty hard-core, each with a number of felonies," she recalls. "At the end of a productive aggression management session, I gave everybody a smiley face sticker except for one kid I chose at random—I was curious about whether he would care or not.

"So I'm packing up and he's kind of hanging around. Finally he says, 'Umm, did you forget anything?' I said, 'No, I don't think so.' And he says, almost pleadingly, 'I didn't get a sticker! Did I do something wrong?'

"'No, no,' I said. 'I just forgot,' and I gave him a sticker. So here's this gang-banger in his early twenties, with a history of arrests a mile long, and he's walking out with a smiley face sticker on his jean jacket like I gave him a brick of gold."

Hanging on when they can't

These stories, however, are often crowded with challenges. That's why, before Waxman walks into a school, probation department, or jail, she reads two phrases taped to the dashboard of her car.

"The first one says 'Observe With Eyes That Honor Kids,'" she says. "If you can truly observe with eyes that honor who these kids can be—who they *want* to be—somewhere along the line you'll get a glimpse of that. And that's when the coolest things can happen for kids.

"The other is 'Offer Dignity in All Ways.' No matter how badly kids act, I can dignify them even while they are facing the consequences of their actions. I think one of the reasons some schools have trouble is because all the staff focuses on is 'What did you do yesterday?' rather than 'What can you do today?' On the other hand, I've also been in schools where the approach is, 'You screwed up Friday and had to face consequences. But today it's Monday and everybody says welcome back and we love you.' That's being there."

Waxman acknowledges that it can be difficult for adults to choose a positive attitude when students are at their worst. "A lot of kids face invisible giants every day—anger at home, racism in the home, poverty. They often behave the way they do because they're emotionally exhausted, and their frustration outweighs their skills. The key, when kids fall short, is to keep it together when they can't. It means reminding yourself, 'I understand the reason you're acting like a jerk is because you're hurting.'"

The flip side, Waxman says, is when adults decide to just make these kids invisible. "When I did my doctoral dissertation, I talked to a dropout. She told me that when she was in school she'd notice teachers in the halls making eye contact with the 'good' kids and saying good morning. She said, 'I don't remember anyone looking me in the eye and saying good morning or thanks for coming.' She dropped out of school at 14 and never showed up again. The thing is, she told me, 'Nobody came to look for me or I would have gone back.'"

Creating a relationship with a student doesn't solve every problem, Waxman acknowledges, but "it does move all issues forward. You almost can't fail if you try to create a positive relationship. In the process we provide a model for them to learn to be kind to people who may not be kind to them."

Waxman says making a student's day by recognizing any positive change is an important first step in building relationships. "A girl in one of my groups dressed like somebody had put a head on top of a pile of clothes. She wore so much black eye makeup I couldn't tell if her eyes were open or closed. But one day she came to group with her shirt tucked in and a barrette in the little bit of her hair that wasn't shaved off. I said to her, 'Wow, you look great today!'

"She stopped walking and just stared at me, just stood there. I said, 'I just told you that you look great. What do you say?'

"She started to cry and she said, 'I don't know. Nobody ever told me that before.'

"After that, this girl would always sit next to me, her shoulder against mine. She would ask to borrow things from me, my pencil or a book to write on. She'd ask if I wanted to braid her hair. She started to care—and all it took was me noticing a small change."

Just go with it

Early in her career, Waxman was working at a youth center when a young man stomped in. He was shaking with an angry look on his face, and he was holding a knife. "Is Joe here?" he asked.

"There were 200 kids with me and three volunteers and I knew Joe was one of them," Waxman recalls. "All I could think of was if I let this kid in, something horrible is going to happen. So I went up to the kid and said, 'Oh, did Joe lose his knife?' Before I knew what I was doing, I took the knife from him and put it in a desk drawer. The kid sat down, shook his head, and said, 'You are the craziest mother _____ I ever met.'"

After 25 years of working with gang members, Waxman admits it occasionally can be dangerous, frustrating, and exhausting. So what has sustained her? "Sometimes all you have left is your sense of humor," she says. "You might as well hang onto it." And, when the situation demands, just go with it.

Waxman was working with a group of sixth graders with behavior disorders. "Summer was approaching and I was suggesting things to do that were alternatives to the street," she says, laughing. "I mentioned a certain park, and this little kid looks at me and says, 'I hurt my nuts at that park.'

"I looked at him—trying to keep from busting out in laughter—as another little kid said, 'You want to know where I hurt *my* nuts?' So I went with it. These kids were completely serious. They weren't guffawing and elbowing each other. One kid would tell where he got hurt, and all the kids would go 'Oooooh!' like they could feel it.

"Somehow I kept from laughing out loud and when we were done, I said, 'Could this discussion happen anywhere?' The class agreed that this subject was probably not appropriate elsewhere in school and I thanked them for their maturity in how they had discussed it.

"Sometime you've just got to Be There with kids, where *they* are," Waxman says. "Besides, they just made me laugh. When you can't enjoy young people, if you can't laugh during the journey, your days are going to be long."

> "Sometimes all you have left is your sense of humor."

Staying rock solid

Rewards like these, Waxman says, are worth the effort. "I have new energy every day, I get to see kids overcome great odds and grow up. Like a girl who used to get in fights every day. She became a police officer and was named Officer of the Year.

"Or, there was the kid, incredibly racist, whose dad was a white supremacist. It took years but he became friends with African-American and Hispanic kids. He was finally able to separate what he believes from what his dad believes. He may not be a kid who's going to college, but he cares about people, lives The FISH! Philosophy, and will contribute, no matter what kind of job he has."

At the end of each group, to celebrate this, Waxman gives the graduates a symbol of their progress. "I give them a river stone," she says. "And I'll say something like, 'You're rock solid' or 'You've been steady.'" This simple gesture has long-term effects.

"A few years ago," Waxman smiles, "a kid comes running up to me and says, 'Do you remember me?!' He reaches in his pocket and pulls out a rock. 'When you said I was rock solid, that's when I finally figured it out—it's totally up to me,' he said. 'Sometimes I'd screw up, but every time I came to your group I was *rock solid* and if I could do it there, I could do it in the rest of my life. As long as I have this reminder, I *can* do it.'"

Children need models rather than critics.

—John Ruskin

 **THOUGHT**

PLANTING SEEDS

Every teacher has plenty of former students who always seemed destined for success. But what about those who, years later, scarcely resemble your memory of them? The sullen, withdrawn boy who now shines as a performer ... the girl whose rebelliousness once frustrated you but whose breathtaking art now touches you ... the student who didn't always care about crafting paragraphs but today crafts furniture with incredible passion and skill.

We will have students who are at times troubled, challenging, or unmotivated, who despite our best efforts seem beyond our help or reach. Yet without us planting the seeds of patience, encouragement, and hopefulness, they may not be ready to bloom when the time is right.

All we can do is be there for them today. Tomorrow will take care of itself.

"It Means No One Ever Has to Be Alone"

When Chris Streiff, the teacher from Gage Elementary School in Rochester, Minnesota, brought The FISH! Philosophy into her classroom, her experience did not go overlooked. "People noticed she was happier," says principal Ann Clark. "They saw her kids becoming more responsible."

Chris shared what she was doing at a staff meeting, and a few colleagues visited her room, but, initially, it didn't go much further than that. "Staff liked The FISH! Philosophy, but they saw it more as a way to pick *each other* up," Ann says. "They didn't see a way to bring it into their classrooms."

Over the next year, however, Gage's challenges grew. The district instituted boundary changes that distributed enrollment and diversity evenly throughout all its schools. Many new students were the children of immigrants, some from war-torn countries like Bosnia and Somalia. Nearly a quarter of Gage's students did not speak, or were learning, English. The free and reduced lunch population doubled to almost 50 percent.

Ann says, "Some of the children had never been in a school. They didn't know how to hold a pair of scissors, had never colored, had never stood in line, or sat at a desk. When one little girl came to us in kindergarten, the only word we could understand was her name. She scored 1 out of a possible 163 on an opening day assessment."

At the same time, Gage's teachers were also asked to implement new curriculum. Testing requirements increased too. "Usually by mid-October, teachers are getting into a routine, but they were telling me, 'We're just not there,'" Ann says. "They wondered what they were doing wrong. They were working hard, but were really down."

That's when several Gage teachers decided they needed a change. "Any time you try something new, it's a leap of faith," Ann says. "Sometimes people just need to watch others first before they give it a shot. Other times you're at the end of your rope and you figure, 'I have to try something different.'"

This time, the "something different" was The FISH! Philosophy.

No one is ever alone

For Amy Amsden, a kindergarten teacher at Gage, The FISH! Philosophy matched her own philosophies. "FISH! is about better relationships," she says. "I'm the first adult my students deal with regularly in school. That's why it's so important for the class to spend the first few weeks establishing a family. Once that's set, everything falls into place."

Still, several months into the school year, Amy felt she didn't have time for "one more thing." Besides, having set her class routine already, Amy wasn't sure how well her students would really understand The FISH! Philosophy. "I told Chris Streiff, 'They're not going to get it. They're only in kindergarten.' Chris said, 'You might be surprised.'"

Amy thought about it: If her kids *did* understand it, maybe FISH! could help with other demands too. "They have to be reading by the end of the year and it really forces me to pick up the pace," Amy says. "These children need academics, but they also need the social component, and we're taking away the time needed for that. FISH! helped us."

The external changes were minimal (Amy made only two changes to her room: she bought a stuffed fish and put up a poster). Internally, however, the classroom transformed.

Amy says, "Before, the children had hung around with the same friends. But once we started practicing The FISH! Philosophy, they made more of an effort to make sure everyone was included. One day, I asked the class what it means to Be There for somebody. A little girl raised her hand and said, 'It means we don't ever want anybody to be alone.'"

These sentiments blossomed into major Make Their Day moments. "On the morning of Valentine's Day, as everyone was arriving at school," Amy explains, "two students wanted to talk to me privately in the hall. Their parents were with them. The students had brought valentines and candy for their classmates who never had money for snacks. Their parents said the kids thought of doing this on their own, and they didn't want anyone to know they were doing this. They just wanted to make sure everyone felt a part of the day."

"They didn't want anyone to know they were doing this."

Shared responsibility

The more the class talked about concepts like Make Their Day, the less Amy worried about controlling every aspect of the classroom. "In the past I had been fanatical about doing it all. I'd stay every night after school until 5 o'clock making sure I did every little thing so we were ready for tomorrow. But I learned that they were very capable of contributing to the classroom environment."

For example, Amy made up an activity called silent vacuum cleaners. "At the end of the day, when we clean up after ourselves, the kids like to crawl on the floor pretending they're silent vacuum cleaners. They pick up the bigger scraps of construction paper we've used because the custodian can't pick them up with a real vacuum. It just takes a minute, the kids love it, and they are proud to take responsibility for themselves."

Soon, making people's day became almost automatic — even when Amy wasn't around. "When they had a substitute, the sub would tell me how thoughtful and appreciative they were. The presence of what we had done through The FISH! Philosophy was still in the room, even if I wasn't. That made me so proud."

This thoughtfulness and choice continued throughout the entire year, Amy concludes. "We used the same attitude survey Chris had created, and one day I circled the sad face. The kids were all over that. 'Miss Amsden, what's wrong?' I told them, 'I'm sad because someone hurt my feelings at noon.' They all tried to make me feel better and then they said, 'Miss Amsden, it's all over with now. You can choose to forgive and move on.' I think they definitely got The FISH! Philosophy."

What do you need today?

Down the hall, this new perspective also inspired Lee Gilmore as she returned to the classroom after 10 years as a Gage Title I reading teacher.

"I saw the importance of being there for kids," she says. "I often worked with students who got the best of nothing. Their bed was a sofa in the living room. When the TV got shut off, *that's* when bedtime was. One day, we closed school at 10:30 a.m. because of a blizzard. Even I enjoy snow days, but one student didn't look too excited. 'Can I please eat in the cafeteria before I leave?' he asked. 'Because I won't get lunch when I get home.'

"My first concern with students was, 'How are you doing? What do you need today?' Without that, we weren't going to get anywhere."

Lee had known about The FISH! Philosophy for years, and actually introduced it to the banker who presented it to Gage. "But when the school took it on," she notes, "I just sat back and watched. Being a Title I teacher, I didn't think I could do FISH! knowing that it wasn't always happening in the classrooms the students were coming from."

All this changed when a new reading program required Lee to return to teaching full time. "I had taught for 10 years, then took a few years off when I had children," she shares. "When my own children were three and five, I went back to the classroom. I tried to be everything to everyone—the perfect mom and the teacher I was before I had children. I had a nervous breakdown and was diagnosed with bipolar disorder. It took me three years before I could go into a school building. I started half time as a Title I reading teacher, then gradually into full time."

Despite her success as a Title I teacher, Lee says she was "scared to death" to go back into the classroom full time. "I shared my fears with Ann and Kevin (assistant principal), found a lot of support from others, and decided to try."

With their help, she also dove into The FISH! Philosophy. "Our class did Stinky Fish and developed a mission statement. We spent five to 10 minutes at the beginning of each day talking about how to Be There for each other. We sang along to a CD of FISH! songs."

With this, Lee and her kids created a safe place for *everyone* to be together. "One of the mothers was bringing in her little girl, who had gone to school in a small town nearby that had little diversity. She said offhandedly, 'Gee, she's never had a class with students who aren't white,'" Lee recalls. "I said, 'Well, what we have here is the real world.' It was wonderful—and the only way I'd teach. The kids celebrated their uniqueness. Unless they've been taught otherwise, they see it as a plus.

"We had a great year," she says. "My proudest moment was watching them walk out the door on the last day of school, knowing how they walked in. They came to me so fragile and frightened, clinging to mom and dad's skirts or legs. When they left, they had some great tools for succeeding in

"It took me three years before I could go into a school building."

life. I asked them, 'Is FISH! something we do just in first grade?' They said, 'No! We can do it all our lives!'"

Lee also took FISH! home to her family: "My husband loves to play golf," she muses. "One day he asked me, 'Do they have FISH! head covers? Because I'd like one for my driver ... I'm trying to change some things in my life and I think it would help, because the place where my attitude is the worst is at the golf course.'"

Principal's principles

While Gage teachers were going strong, Gage principal Ann Clark was diving into her own version of FISH!

"My job is almost exclusively problem solving," she says. "They sent a student to my office who's late all the time. His mom never gets up. We got him an alarm clock and taught him to use it. He's in second grade. Sometimes we have to teach life skills first so they can be here to get the academics."

"Sometimes we have to teach life skills so they can be here for the academics."

She continues, "We had one little guy who wasn't turning in his homework. He and the social worker finally figured out a way for him to get it done: His household is really noisy so he goes into the bathroom. It's the only place in the house where it's quiet and that's where he does his homework. He calls it his office."

While FISH! helps create solutions, Ann notes, being there and making someone's day doesn't automatically mean solving their problem *for* them. "Occasionally, when staff would come to me with a concern, they just wanted me to solve it. But I'd rather listen and help them think through what works for *them*. So we'd brainstorm three ideas to try. Nine times out of 10, they'd figure it out on their own. Every once in a while they'd come back, write out the three ideas, and ask me to pick one."

This method helps teachers look at conflicts from the other person's perspective. She continues, "Often, when educators come down hard on students, we perceive that we are really helping them. But it really doesn't matter to the child what *your* perspective is; what matters to them is how *they* perceive it.

"The key to discipline is creating a win-win situation. If the child perceives it's a losing situation, it may seem that you win today. But they may give up, act out, or detach. And if they don't like coming to class anymore, then you lose too."

A teaching opportunity

Gage assistant principal Kevin Ewing agrees. With discipline problems, he says, FISH! presents teaching opportunities: "It used to be that the rules at home were pretty much the rules at school, but that's shifted. In more and more students' lives, if a kid messes up, it's either ignored or unseen. When the parent *does* react, the reaction may be over the top—screaming, even hitting. Kids learn that "if I'm caught I'll deny it." If the adult is angry enough, "I'll get it, but then they'll feel bad and I'll go right back to where I was." Nowhere in that loop is a teaching opportunity.

"Without that teaching opportunity," he continues, "crime and punishment doesn't work. Kids feel bad about being punished. They feel bad they're missing recess. They feel bad they're washing tables because they threw food. But they don't feel bad about actually *committing the act*. The key is not for me to solve it for them, but for them to acknowledge it, understand it, and resolve it so it doesn't happen again."

Kevin feels The FISH! Philosophy helps this process. "FISH! presents some real ownership opportunities to practice behaviors that will keep kids from making poor decisions—choosing my attitude, making their day. If someone's calling me a name or shoving me, how do I choose to respond?"

This choice is key for Kevin, who handles many of Gage's most serious discipline issues. "On my computer screen saver I have a fish and the words Choose Your Attitude written by one of the kids I saw the most for behavior issues. I always remember that. When I go out to see a kid or walk around the school, I think, 'What kind of person do I want the kids to see?' I may not be teaching in the classroom, but I am in a teaching mode all day."

Once challenging, this is now a simple habit for Kevin. He continues, "I typically get to know the kids who are the frequent flyers the best. I want to know *all* the kids, but on the other hand, the frequent flyers are the kids who need my help right now. That's how I can be there. There are so many kids who may be aggravating today but deserve and *need* our time. Even if I don't always see results right away, I believe what I'm doing is an investment that will pay a dividend in the future."

A can-do spirit

As FISH! planted this seed of possibility throughout Gage in the spring of 2004, it wasn't only the teachers and administrators who were jazzed. The support staff was especially excited. "A music teacher told me, 'I see 27 sections of students twice in a six-day cycle,'" Ann says. "In the past, every teacher had a different behavior plan and used different words. Now I'm going to be able to say something and they'll know what I'm talking about. We'll all be on the same page."

"That's so important," Kevin adds. "At a retirement banquet, I heard people talk about their own school experiences. They said the most important person in their life at school was a cook or a custodian. It might be the nurse a student goes to every day to get his inhaler. It could be a secretary or playground supervisor. Any one of these people might be the person with whom a kid creates a relationship, feels comfortable talking to."

As they moved through the year, evidence showed this school-wide emphasis on relationships paying off. "We've seen a decrease in behavior incidents," Kevin says. "That's due to some specific behavior strategies, but also because more staff are thinking FISH!"

Which led to more students thinking about it as well. Second grade teacher Shayna Woodburn knew she was making progress with one of her most challenging students when she saw him explaining The FISH! Philosophy to another teacher. "Another day in class, when we were talking about a poor choice someone had made," she recalls, "a boy said, 'If you do that, you're not making their day, you're breaking their day!'"

These student-driven discipline changes also translated into impressive academic gains. In a report measuring the reading progress of students between third and fifth grade, Gage ranked second among 15 schools in the district. "The staff was amazing," Ann says. "I know they were exhausted, continually having to think up plan after plan to make things work for their students, but they kept coming back every day with a smile on their faces.

"And our students made so much progress. The little girl who started the year with just 1 out of 163 on her assessment ended the year with 150. I think of all the kids who were so far behind who are now reading at grade level.

"Of course," she emphasizes, "because standardized tests don't measure where students start at, only where they end up, we're constantly under pressure. Still, this staff has a strong feeling that we're not stuck with no place to go. We *will* figure it out. We *will* find a way."

Ann says, "When you're down, FISH! is not a program or curriculum that keeps your 'spirits up.' FISH! is about how we choose to treat other people. It's a language that reminds us why we became teachers in the first place. It helps us focus on what really matters.

"If you wanted to get technical," she adds, "you could call FISH! 'a strategy to create the culture that needs to exist to provide optimal student learning.' Or you could just say it helps us take care of each other."

"All the kids are reading at grade level."

"Good People Are Waiting for You"

This is a story about socks that doubled as mittens, a tractor, a squirrel in a book bag, and a boy who picked up pennies for luck.

It's about what happens when life *away* from school intersects with life *at* school; about how even the pain you bring from home can be a strength when you know you're not alone. It's about how important it is to enter each new day ready to care for one another, not just when times are tough, but when they're good. It's about what students can learn from adults who model caring relationships. It's about what Be There looks like.

Stories like this can happen at any school, but this one happened at Buchanan Elementary in Pierre, South Dakota.

Life is good

Paula Stout loved her first graders. She loved the way they came wanting to learn the world in a matter of days. She loved the way their excited eyes shouted "Thank you!" when they learned something new.

When Paula needed the children's attention, she would step on a stool and ask them to take their seats. When Mrs. Stout went to her chair, students knew it was time to go to theirs. If their pencil lead broke, she'd direct them to the magic pencil on her desk. When kids forgot their mittens—or didn't have any—she'd take out the sock box, let them pick the color they wanted, and wear them on their hands at recess. "They loved the sock box. When you put a coat over them," she smiles, "nobody knows they're not mittens."

"They loved the sock box."

Some of Paula's kids had hard lives, and sometimes so many clouds built up inside that it had to rain. "One boy had a brother who had been abusive before being removed from the home," she says. "Sometimes this little guy let out his frustrations by being very aggressive and when he calmed down, he wouldn't even realize what had happened."

Paula would talk gently with her class about how instead of focusing on how he had just acted, they could help him by being his friend and easing his hurt. "They were so understanding. When the boy came back to the room, his classmates would go to him and help him get back to his happy self."

Paula loved helping her kids. And when the day was done, she loved being with her husband, David. An employee of the Department of Game, Fish and Parks, David loved being outdoors and spending time on the river. "I was born 100 years too late," he'd laugh. At night, David would carve wooden decoys while Paula worked on her own hobbies. She often stopped and just sat and watched him work, and he'd look at her contentedly.

Your kids need you

One October morning, like so many before, David kissed Paula and headed to work. A few minutes later he called on his cell phone with the news no wife wants to hear. "I blacked out and had an accident," he said.

Paula rushed to the scene, a few blocks away.

"The police were there and an ambulance was on the way," she says. "He kept saying he wasn't hurt from the accident, but he said his head hurt." It turned out a blood vessel in his brain had burst. David died later that day.

Paula was lost. How do you find your way without your best friend? Her family surrounded her, but afterward she didn't want to leave her house. She didn't want to *do* anything.

Her family at school wasn't sure how to help. "We didn't know how to make her feel better," recalls Renee Flakus, who taught first grade with Paula. "I couldn't say I knew how she felt, because I didn't. All we could do is Be There for her. We brought her favorite ice cream, Rocky Road. If she wanted to talk, we listened. If she wanted to sit, we sat with her."

Buchanan principal Dan Cronin gently reminded her that she still had an important purpose. "Your kids need you, Paula," he said. "They love Mrs. Stout and they need you …. If you need us, we're here."

Over time, Paula knew he was right. "I had to focus on my kids. They had their whole lives ahead of them. I had to make sure they knew what they were supposed to know before they moved on."

Three weeks after David's death, Paula bravely returned to Buchanan, half days at first. "My class was so excited to see me I don't know if they really understood what had happened. But they picked up on what I was feeling. They hugged me a lot more than usual."

So did her colleagues. Dan was always there to talk, and the other teachers and aides looked after her. "Sometimes I'd pop into the classroom, the kids would be working, and she'd be sitting at her desk, lost in her thoughts," Renee recalls. "I'd say, 'Paula, do you need some time? Your kids can come over with mine.' Usually she'd say, 'Oh, I'm fine.' Other days, she'd need to leave for a few minutes."

Day by day, things got easier for Paula. She couldn't yet bring out the turtle shell and beaver skull David had given her to use in her animal unit,

"If she wanted to talk, we listened. If she wanted to sit, we sat with her."

but she knew she would someday. A few months later, when the Department of Game, Fish and Parks dedicated 700 acres of wetlands to David's memory, it seemed to Paula that every bird within miles chose that moment to fly over the site. "He would have liked that," Paula says.

A balanced life

Through it all, Paula taught two doors down from Renee Flakus—who had been such a personal and professional support. "Renee was younger than I was, so excited and enthusiastic," Paula says. "That rubbed off on all of us, like we can do it too."

Renee drew her energy from her first graders. She was always reading, taking classes, looking for even better ways to deliver her lessons. She drew on her experience teaching on a reservation to connect with her Native American students, who made up about 20 percent of the school's population.

Renee worked hard to make class safe by helping her young students put themselves in others' shoes. "I felt like the best way to come together was to talk about our differences. We talked about how each of us like different colors and animals. We'd discuss how a character in a book might feel differently about something than we did, and why that was okay. The more the kids learned to accept others, the more they knew they were going to be accepted—that made it easier to learn."

Renee was flexible. "If we were on a topic, and students got interested in something, we'd go with it," she says. "I figured it was more important to feed their enthusiasm. We'd get books on the topic or get on the Internet and research it."

This flexibility followed her outside of school as well, where, 13 miles away, she and her husband, Ron, owned a ranch with 400 head of cattle. "Every day I'd get on my coveralls and boots and help with chores," she says.

It seemed to Paula that every bird within miles chose that moment to fly over the site.

"Afterward I'd be reading something related to teaching and I'd fall asleep, exhausted. But if it was calving season, I might be up every few hours helping or bringing a newborn calf into our bathtub to warm her up so she didn't turn into an icicle."

When Renee told these stories at school, the teachers would laugh and say, "You don't look like a cowgirl!"

"But I'm hatching chicks tomorrow!"

In late April 2001, Ron and Renee were feeding cattle. Ron drove the tractor, as Renee stood on the side, hopping on and off to open pasture gates. Every night they repeated this routine safely. But *this* night, Renee slipped and fell.

The back wheel of the tractor, weighing thousands of pounds, rolled directly over the right side of her head and body. Ron, scrambling to stop the tractor, clambered to her side. Renee was conscious enough to hear him screaming. He picked her up and started running, but her pain was too much. "No!" she screamed. Ron set her down, quickly wrapped a sweatshirt around her bleeding head, and ran to get the four-wheeler. He laid her across it and sped back through the same pasture gates Renee had just opened.

"You don't look like a cowgirl."

When he got Renee in the car, Ron called 911 as he started driving. The dispatcher told Ron he'd send an ambulance. As Renee wheezed, Ron screamed, "No, we're coming!" As they neared Pierre, a police escort with siren wailing cleared traffic as they raced for the hospital. Ron carried Renee into the emergency room.

Renee had several cracked ribs. One had punctured her lung. The pain was so great she had no idea the tractor tire had peeled the skin off her scalp from her right ear to the top of her head. The doctors quickly decided to fly her to Sioux Falls, a few hours away, for internal and plastic surgery.

Before they lifted off, doctors and nurses worked to stabilize her. Renee's focus, however, was oddly different: "I have to get back to school tomorrow!" she gasped. "I'm hatching chicks in my room!"

A friend in need

Ron called Paula immediately to tell her Renee wouldn't be at school the next day. Paula said she'd be right there. "Everything was so painful, but I was worried about Paula," Renee remembers. "I didn't want her reliving everything with Dave. I kept saying, 'Are you okay?'" Paula was okay, and she stayed with Renee until she was airlifted out.

Immediately, the support came flooding in. Cards and flowers from her colleagues and students filled Renee's hospital room. One first grader, who was very close to Renee, was so upset she told her mother, "If we had known that was Mrs. Flakus's last day, we could have had a party for her."

Yet, already, Renee had no intention of *not* coming back. Principal Dan Cronin assured her that there was no rush. "You have to take care of yourself," he said. "You take the time you need." Renee kept insisting she'd be back at school before the end of the year. That was less than a month and a half away.

Released from the hospital six days later, Renee told everyone on the phone that she was fine, but her outer confidence was greater than what she was feeling inside. When she saw her stitches running from her ear to the top of her head, she was horrified. She broke down and cried.

Over the next few weeks, people stepped forward to help. Family members took care of the ranch and neighbors did chores. The father of one of Renee's students helped with calving—during a late spring blizzard.

Paula was there too. Something happened that brought her out of her depression. "It was time for me to Be There for somebody. I was needed."

"It was a really hard time for Ron and me," Renee recalls. "He was saying, 'We're getting out of this business. I can't go through this again.' Paula took our minds off that. She told us what was happening at school, how my students were doing. She fed us. She brought treats for my cats."

The scars on Renee's face were a long way from healing and the smallest cough sent agonizing pain throughout her cracked ribs, but she grew stronger. Paula said it was because she had carried all those heavy buckets of cattle feed. On May 8, three weeks after the accident, Renee drove herself to school and walked into her classroom. Dan Cronin, Paula, and many other teachers were waiting. There were many joyful tears.

"Dan had a sub for me, so for a while I just enjoyed being back," Renee says. "I moved pretty slow and I looked a wreck, but the kids didn't say one word about my face. They were just happy to see me."

Learning how to teach at home

The South Dakota summer brought warmth and healing to the entire community. By September, teachers and students geared up for another year at Buchanan. Everyone was glad to be back, especially Paula and Renee—and their colleague, Mary Crawford.

Mary had been teaching for more than 20 years, and there had been a time when she wasn't so excited. "I was in an unhappy marriage and I was unhappy at home. I didn't know how to fix it and I brought that to school with me," she says. "I wish I could go back and change things."

But, Mary had discovered she could choose the way she approached her sixth grade class, even as a single mother. Her son Brady helped her make that choice.

Brady was, in Mary's words, a free spirit. "I picked him up once in second grade. He jumped in the car, looked at me and I looked at him, and finally he said, 'Well, what's so bad about having a dead squirrel in your book bag?'

"I wish I could go back and change things."

"That kid was so generous. He'd save his money and buy me flowers just to make my day. As he got older, we learned that when people would compliment him on a shirt or a sweater, he'd give it to them the next day. I guess his dad talked with him about *that*," she smiles.

While Brady was full of joy and exuberance, he and school did not get along. "He had AD/HD and Oppositional Defiant Behavior Disorder— a heck of a mix," she says. "He was very creative but school was a struggle for him. He had an aversion to pencils and any activity that required one. I would teach all day and at night I'd end up fighting with him to do his homework. All I could do was sit with him and Be There."

Being there for Brady helped Mary in the classroom. "I never had such compassion for kids who struggled in school until I had this child. I learned you have to be a little more patient, because if you didn't stick with them, they'd end up hating school like my son did. The more positive I was, the better results I got."

The food patrol

Then, early in the morning of October 12, Mary got the call.

"It was my ex-husband. Brady was living with him at the time in North Dakota. There had been a crash. Brady was in a car with two girls and two other boys. None of them was wearing seat belts and Brady had been critically injured."

Mary rushed to the hospital in Bismarck. The doctors could not save him. Brady died at 3:15 that afternoon. He was 17.

Three carloads of teachers from Buchanan came to the funeral, led by principal Dan Cronin. When Mary returned home, she had little appetite, so teachers brought food and stayed with her to make sure she ate it. "I called them the food patrol." She smiles softly. Dan and his wife, who lived across the street, came over all the time to see how she was doing. And the whole staff rallied together once again to support one of their own. After a few weeks, Mary decided to come back to school.

Bringing it all into focus

Shortly after Brady's death, Mary learned about The FISH! Philosophy. One of its pillars is that you can Choose Your Attitude. Just getting up in the morning was painful, but something about that idea kept her going.

"You wouldn't wish the pain on anyone," Mary says. "But I believed God had sent me this child to make me a better teacher and now it was time to go back and start *being* that teacher.

"I told my class they were going to be with a woman who was going to cry, and that was okay with them." The idea of Be There also resonated with her, and she found herself comforting people who were crying for *her*.

Mary shared The FISH! Philosophy with Dan Cronin, who gladly introduced it to the staff. "After what had happened with Paula, Renee, and Mary, it was easy for us as a staff to talk about The FISH! Philosophy," he says. "We had seen that when we're there for each other, we could get through anything. We'd seen each other at our best in tough times. What if we could be that way *all* the time?

"FISH! reminded us of what we were trying to do for our students, parents, and community," Dan adds. As the staff got behind it, he'd often send e-mails as a reminder, ending each one with, "Don't forget to go fishing!" A teacher recalls, "It would always get you thinking, 'Oh yeah, *that's* why we're here.'"

Buchanan had always had a pleasant environment, but Paula noticed people taking more time for one another. "It might be the worst Monday in the world, but you still wanted to get to work because you knew there were good people there waiting for you."

"I told my class they were going to be with a woman who was going to cry, and that was okay with them."

Laughing through it all

While some days were easier, others still posed challenges. In response, Mary had ideas to bring laughter back to the school.

"If one of us was feeling down, we'd call for a Bead Day," she says. "Some days we'd wear 10 to 12 strands of Mardi Gras beads. They looked ridiculous. And people would ask, 'Why are you wearing those beads?' We'd tell them, 'Oh, just because it's Tuesday.'"

On the 100th day of the school year, Mary and her partners dressed up as 100-year-old ladies. "We told our kids to dress that way too." She decorated the teacher's lounge. If she saw someone acting a little cranky, she'd buy a little gift and leave it in their mailbox. "You can buy the dorkiest stuff for a dollar." She grins.

"Mary's loss was still pretty recent," Dan says. "A lot of times as coworkers you don't know how to deal with others' tragedies. She opened the door to make it easier to laugh with her."

Mary agreed. "I just healed better when I got back to school. There was a whole bunch of love there. We'd catch each other doing cool things and saying, 'Hey that was a neat lesson you did.' Or 'Your kids did really great with their play.' We didn't take things for granted. We looked out for each other. We didn't leave as many compliments unsaid."

"Did you ever wonder where people went to the bathroom in castles?"

While the teachers experimented, Mary also made it safe for students to take more risks with learning by modeling the way. "After FISH!, I was a lot more willing to take a leap and know the net is there. My kids know they can ask any question because I bring up the goofiest things myself. When we studied ancient civilizations, I asked, 'Did you ever wonder where people went to the bathroom in castles?' Of course, they looked at me like, 'Sure, we wonder, but we're not supposed to bring that up.'" (For the record, according to Mary, the castles had recessed, built-in toilets connected to a gutter that hung out over the moat.)

Mary continued to open up, and to let her students get to know her.

"We did an exercise called *Top 10 Things to Know About Me*. I mentioned that my son had died, and it wasn't uncomfortable at all. They wanted to know more about him, to share my grief. That makes a difference because sixth grade can be tough. Some days some kids decide to hate me and other days they can't get close enough. What keeps them coming back is our relationship."

"It's your lucky day"

No one at Buchanan knew how to choose his attitude better than Robert did. Now a fifth grader in Katrina Mosteller's class, he had been diagnosed with cancer in first grade. His mother talked to his classmates about what cancer was, how they couldn't catch it, and how they shouldn't treat him any differently. And they didn't. To them, he was just Robert.

When Robert's chemotherapy treatments temporarily took his light brown hair, he wore a baseball hat. But it didn't take away his smile, which stretched from ear to ear.

Robert loved sports. Though the cancer weakened his muscles, he always wanted to play. The other boys figured out that if he stood close to the goal line, they could throw the football to him and he'd score.

"Though the cancer weakened his muscles, he always wanted to play."

Robert brought that same energy to the classroom. "He was almost like my teacher's aide," Katrina says. "He was so excited to learn that it rubbed off on other kids, even me. He was very intelligent. He asked lots of questions I didn't know the answers to. I'd say, 'You stumped me again, Robert!' It was great for kids to see that the teacher doesn't know all the answers and that you learn all through life. So we'd look up the answers together. He loved airplanes, the stock market, Greek mythology. He'd go in depth into whatever he was studying, and he always wanted to know more.

"Because of Robert, the kids saw you don't ever have to be defeated. He was concerned about *other* people. When he came back from treatment in fourth grade, his teacher asked how he was. Robert said, '*I'm* fine. It's my *mom* I'm worried about. She's a nurse and she knows too much!'"

Robert lived with all the strength he had but in fifth grade, the cancer came back stronger. He began to miss school. Summer came and went. When his classmates started sixth grade, he was in a hospital bed. He came home for a few days around Thanksgiving, but he died a few months later.

Robert's funeral reflected how he had lived. "They played his choice of music. One of his selections was 'The Notre Dame Victory March Song,'" Katrina says. "There were balloons, plants and flowers, a big baseball, basketball, and football. The pastor did a nice job reminding us of all the wonderful things that Robert and his family taught us.

"At the end of the service he told how Robert and his mom, when they'd see a penny, would pick it up for good luck. As we all left the church, they put out baskets of pennies that he and his mom had collected over the years. Robert left instructions that we all take a penny, because every day is lucky."

Forever connected

Life goes on and life changes.

Dan Cronin took on a new assignment as principal at Jefferson Elementary in Pierre. On his last day at Buchanan, the teachers performed a FISH! skit and gave him a large plastic fish. "I learned how important relationships are," Dan says. "If you have trust and support, you can accomplish anything. I can't believe I ever took that for granted. It takes time and now I'm working on building that in my new school."

Renee set off on a new adventure too. She and Ron sold their cattle business and moved to Las Vegas so Renee could pursue her master's degree in early literacy teaching. "Renee was always enthusiastic but after the accident she became a real leader," Dan says. "She had such drive and determination to help kids learn. Everything she did was so purposeful."

Paula helped Renee move, and they still talk regularly. Paula stayed at Buchanan, where she continued to put socks on her students' hands and learning in their hearts. She missed David terribly, but she was finally able to take out the beaver skull and turtle shell he gave her to teach her animal unit. She also started carving ducks.

Occasionally, Paula's first graders would ask about the picture of the boy on her wall, and she would tell them about Robert. Robert has a tree at Buchanan, and when they dedicated it, they threw pennies and made wishes.

Mary moved to Georgia Morse Middle School and found a group of like-minded teachers to laugh with and tease at lunch, leaving refreshed for another afternoon of learning.

"I have a good day every day," she says. "Some days are better than others, but when I walk in my classroom and the kids scream, 'Good morning!' I just really like being with them. I was thinking the other day about how I used to wear my Mardi Gras beads when I was feeling down. I haven't worn them in a while—I must be having a pretty happy patch in my life."

Oh, and she got married again. "I had been seeing him for 11 years. After Brady died I realized life is too short, so I just took the day off and we got hitched. Pretty cool."

"She was finally able to take out the beaver skull."

PLAY

PLAY

PLAY

It's not surprising why people are drawn to Play. When we're having a great time, we're energized. When we're enjoying ourselves, we're in the moment. Psychologists say fun is a basic human need, right up with having a sense of control over one's life and the need to be loved. So what's keeping us from playing more at school? 🐟 One reason is the belief that work and play have no common ground. Play is often associated with laziness or frivolity, and work with serious pursuits. This mindset dictates that too much fun only distracts students from the effort and concentration that learning demands. In this mindset, Play gets in the way. Fun becomes foe. 🐟 Play, however, has nothing to do with laziness. Watch kids in a basketball game, creating elaborate dramas, doing an art project. They aren't taking it easy. Play is when students are trying their hardest, giving it their all. Play is when they're achieving, accomplishing, and excelling. Play is when they're focused and having fun.

Finding this fun In The FISH! Philosophy, Play is not limited to activities separate from work. Instead, work and Play are interdependent, each necessary to create those magic moments where real learning occurs. 🐟 In this mindset, then, the issue becomes: How do we unearth such moments? 🐟 A good place to begin is to pull out your fear-o-meter.

It's hard for students to find a spirit of Play if fear exists in the classroom—fear of making mistakes, of violating rules, of being judged for being different. Sometimes teachers are fearful too. They wonder: If I encourage too playful an atmosphere, will my colleagues still take me seriously? Am I somehow condoning inappropriate behavior? Will I get yelled at? Focusing on all four FISH! Philosophy principles will help you find an appropriate "playing field." For example, if you tell jokes that offend others, or goof around when people are talking to you, you are not being there. If you Play in a way that excludes others or makes fun at their expense, you are not making their day. If your Play is negative or sarcastic, you are not choosing an attitude of openness and lightheartedness. But when Play happens in a context of Be There, Make Their Day, and Choose Your Attitude, it will be appropriate and productive. In the process, classmates learn to trust and respect each other in a way that makes it safe to take risks with learning. Play occurs naturally, genuinely —and fear gets the boot. In its place comes curiosity, enthusiasm, creativity, and, often, higher-level thinking. It's important to remember that not everyone has fun in the same way, and it's critical to honor those who "Play" so quietly or subtly that it may not seem like Play at all. You can't force people to Play, but you can *free* them to play.

"It's My Job to Care"

On her first day as an intern teacher, Kristin Puntenney missed her alarm, was delayed by construction, got lost, and walked in late to a professional development session at Amelia High School. The only seat left was in the front row.

The presenter noticed her right away. "You have now missed what everyone else already knows," he roared in mock indignation. He was kidding, but was too good an actor; Kristin could not see a trace of humor anywhere on his face. She felt terrible.

As the morning's frustration welled, Kristin's eyes filled with tears. "I felt like the new kid at camp who everyone labels a crybaby," she recalls. The presenter admitted he'd been joking and felt awful. He offered her candy—"as though sugar could sweeten what he'd done," Kristin chuckles—and asked her colleagues to comfort her.

Later, during a break, some burly teachers told her, "We'll kick his butt if he gets on you again!" Unintentionally, the experience had led them to Be There for her. She felt their support, laughed with them, and started to relax.

As the morning's session continued—a workshop on The FISH! Philosophy—Kristin found herself drawn to the ideas. She opened up and received a stuffed fish for answering questions. She thought about her goals and, at the end of the workshop, filled out a time capsule to be opened four months later as a form of rejuvenation.

By choosing her attitude, Kristin's morning had shifted and became a true learning experience. Before she sealed her envelope, the presenter wrote on the flap, "You are my hero. Thank you."

In a few days, Kristin decided, she would bring The FISH! Philosophy to her first classroom experience.

Reality sets in

As an intern high school French teacher, Kristin had assumed that her students were all excited and motivated. Reality set in when she handed out questionnaires asking why students were in the class. Amidst the few enthusiastic responses, she mostly read about Spanish III being full, or having to take French I because other electives were closed.

Realizing what she was up against, Kristin checked in with FISH! and started to plow ahead.

To better understand her students' learning styles, Kristin asked them to reflect on the way they learned best—so she could help them, in their own ways. To her surprise, they took the task seriously. By trying to get to know them better, Kristin had been there for them. The kids—even those wishing for Spanish III—were impressed.

Kristin's next hurdle was the many students who lacked confidence. New to French, and despite Kristin's encouragement, many would not speak for fear of looking uncool in front of their friends. "I got everybody a mirror, and we made silly faces in the mirror before practicing pronunciation," she says. "They thought it was dumb but it loosened them up so they at least tried." Through Play, Kristin engaged her students to try.

Kristin began to set the tone for each day at the door of her classroom. There her puppet, Pierre le Poisson (Pierre the fish), greeted every student by name as he or she arrived, helping Kristin gauge each student's mood for the day. "Some would respond in French," she says. "Others would chat until the bell rang."

Even more reality

The class started to get into a groove, and trust was established. Kristin soon learned that while several of her students were smart and creative, they were also often preoccupied with worries outside of school.

One student worked after school to support his family; he earned more than his mother did. When the family's water was shut off several times, he was forced to bathe using a jug of water from the supermarket.

Kristin learned that for some of her students' parents, academics were far from a priority; one of her calls to a parent generated little more than a few grunts from the hungover father. Undaunted, Kristin stayed focused on the kids' needs.

"I told them 'You need your brain every day. If you misplace it, let me know. We are not all on, every single day. Lots of things can get in the way, so if you need a day off, tell me.' A few students took me up on this and they never abused the policy. Maybe mom was arrested or boyfriend broke up with girl-friend—whatever the case, as long as they told me, it was okay. Sometimes when kids were sad, I'd give them Pierre for the day. That always helped."

As the year went on, Kristin also realized that some of the kids didn't expect success from themselves, simply because no one had ever expected it of them. Fanned by Kristin's commitment, an ember of hope still glowed. After the first trimester, Kristin asked students, "What more can I do to help you?" One wrote, "Don't give up on me."

> "You need your brain every day. If you misplace it, let me know."

Learn to play, play to learn

Today's students, Kristin notes, are used to being entertained by TV, video games, or the computer. "It doesn't mean they are lazier," she says. "It does mean teaching strategies need to be more engaging."

For Kristin, that meant playing with lesson plans. "Our big project was called the Shop and Swap. Students created a storefront of a food specialty shop in France with awnings, walk-up windows, and display cases. The 'staff' of each store was in charge of bringing in foods: cheese, yogurt, breads, deli meats.

"I gave each student 100 euros to go shopping. As they visited each store, they had to converse in French to get what they wanted. I was watching and they were being graded. It was like playing grocery story when they were little. Mimicking real life makes lessons stick. Plus, the project incorporated all five of Ohio's foreign language standards."

To teach the names of body parts, Kristin put the words of popular songs, such as "The Hokey Pokey," into French and danced with the class. The repetitive movement helped students remember the lessons — as did the goofiness of shaking their arms, legs, and ears. "Creative dramatics, miming, and active learning are all recommended kinesthetic activities for the foreign language classroom," Kristin says.

To encourage even more conversation, "We'd have surprise wine (sparkling grape juice) and cheese parties, but it was also a quiz," she says. "I'd be the party host and students would answer questions during our social rounds, like, 'What are you doing during winter vacation?'"

Different styles

Amelia High School contained five small schools, each designed around a different interest. Kristin taught within the Creative Arts and Design School (CAD) and the School for World Studies (WS). To adjust to each group's learning style, her lesson plans flexed even more as she tuned in to her students' interests.

For example, many of her CAD students had musical, spatial, and kinesthetic intelligence and wouldn't sit still for lectures and historical videos. After discussing the causes of the French Revolution, and contrasting it with the American Revolution, she brought in a CD of the musical *Les Miserables* and the class analyzed its lyrics. "Their essays were the best of the year," Kristin says.

Her other kids—the World Studies students—were most interested in the vocabulary for countries and nationalities. So Kristin assigned each to research a country—the Play way.

"We talked about the stereotypes of each country, and the kids were only too happy to make fun of other countries. But I also assigned them to find three facts that went against the stereotypes. They acted out the stereotypes then gave us the truth. It really changed their attitudes and taught them to be tolerant of others."

Thumbs up

In addition to shaking up the lessons, Kristin brought fun to classroom management. "I wanted enthusiasm but the French II class was almost too enthusiastic," she says. "I never got angry or yelled. I'd try to make eye contact, smile, even say the name of a student if necessary, but it didn't work too well."

She found a more effective technique in a book she was reading about a fifth grade teacher. "When the class is noisy I put my thumb up, then they put their thumbs up. Thumbs up means no talking. It's the same concept as raising a hand, only more playful. It was so effective students often put their thumbs up before I did."

Kristin's French II class, however, was just the opposite. "I couldn't get them to say anything!" Kristin laughs. So at the beginning of class, she'd write the name of one student on paper, fold it, and place it under a magnet where everyone could see it. "If that person participated well during class," she explains, "the entire class would get a prize — usually candy — and I'd reveal the student's name. If the person didn't participate, I didn't reveal the name and the class didn't get the prize. It worked great. The chosen person was always the hero."

Points for discipline

To keep students engaged, Kristin also invented a reward system called P's Points. These were slips of paper with a French word written on them. Students received points for winning a game, giving great answers, trying extra hard. Each slip was worth one point. When you got five points, they could be used as a homework pass. "Colors of points changed each trimester, so old points couldn't carry over ... kind of like a bad cell phone plan," Kristin jokes.

Early in the year, Kristin also decided to stop giving detentions. "They were insignificant to kids," she says. "The ones who got the most always had so many they couldn't serve them all anyway." She did, however, find issue — and success — with three problems: not coming to class prepared, coming to class "incredibly late," or using the word 'gay' to put someone down. "Every time one of those things happened, students lost P's Points," she says. "It really cut down on those incidents."

When it came to dealing with parents, Puntenney wanted to make sure she not only called home to discuss problems, but also to congratulate students. She sent good-news postcards home, and sometimes she just called parents to tell them about their child's success.

"Some parents were in disbelief when I called," she says. "They said

"Nobody from school has ever called with good news before! Thank you."

things like, 'Are you sure you have the right student?' One said, 'Nobody from school has ever called with good news before! Thank you.'"

Be There inside—and outside—of class

Throughout the year, Kristin took time to cover The FISH! Philosophy with her students—the very thing that inspired her style of teaching. They would rate themselves on how well they lived the philosophy; they rated Kristin as well and gave her ideas on how she could do better. For example, they suggested she no longer check her e-mail during class so she could better Be There for students who needed her.

Kristin also noticed that kids often felt bogged down because teachers sometimes assigned major projects at the same time. "I asked if certain due dates would work for them," Kristin says. "I was flexible, they appreciated it, and they didn't abuse it. When they felt I was listening, they were more likely to comply anyway."

Despite such efforts, one student still refused to work and didn't even bring a book, pen, or paper to class. "He wasn't disruptive, just noncompliant," Kristen says. "I could have punished him, but instead I gave him a pen and paper every day and made him use my book. Sometimes he refused to use the materials, and one time I actually held his hand like a small child and made him write."

"... I actually held his hand like a small child and made him write."

The boy complied, but he looked up and said, "Why do you have to care? None of my other teachers do."

"It's my job to care," Kristin said.

The next day, and every day thereafter, the boy came to class with his materials. He even asked a few pertinent questions. "His grade didn't improve right away, but he knew I wasn't going to give up," Kristin says. "After failing the first two trimesters, he got a B- in the last trimester."

Kristin also found ways to Be There for her students outside class. When the web design class e-mailed Amelia teachers begging for biographical information for their web site, she was one of only five who responded, and it helped them complete a successful project.

She also found she enjoyed attending after-school events. She chaperoned a field trip to the Renaissance Festival, where she hung out with the special ed kids and had a blast. She went to musicals, games, and contests, and inevitably left feeling proud of the students' talents and effort.

"I always wondered where the joy of children goes after they outgrow their cute stage," she wrote in a college paper describing her first year of teaching. "I now know it exists in their accomplishments."

An incredible year

Kristin took this lesson—and so many others—to heart during her first year teaching. And, at a second workshop in March 2004, when she saw the presenter who had made her cry, it all came full circle.

"His jaw dropped to the floor. He couldn't believe I came back," she says. "It was nice to see him again. I wanted to show him that I was living what he had taught me. I had the most incredible year as an intern—I hope it's not the peak of my career," she laughs.

"I don't know if The FISH! Philosophy is going to be in my next school," she says. "But it will be in my classroom."

The great thing
in this world is
not so much where
we stand, as in
what direction we
are moving.

—Oliver Wendell Holmes

 **THOUGHT**

HONEST QUESTIONS

In the *FISH!* video, one of the fishmongers admits, "I spent a lot of years rolling my eyes when people asked me questions ... and how could they be so stupid as to ask me a question somebody else asked me 10 minutes earlier. If I was going to be honest with myself, that person that just asked me the same question I heard 10 minutes earlier doesn't even know that person from 10 minutes ago. They are just honestly asking me a question."

There is nothing more important in the classroom than an honest question, asked out of nothing more than the sincere desire to learn. How we respond sets the tone of our school. Will we roll our eyes (literally or figuratively) or will we Be There?

Focus on the curiosity behind the asking, not your experience of answering, and it may lead everyone in the class to new discoveries. Compete with your students to see who can be most inquisitive, and continually replenish your own sense of wonder.

"But You're a Girl"

The first time Eileen Ervine invited a student to play catch outside, he eyed her suspiciously. "You can't throw a football," he said. "You're a girl."

"Let's go find out," she said. "I whipped out my sneakers, threw my heels in the closet, and away we went. When he saw I could throw a spiral, he couldn't believe it. The word spread pretty fast: The assistant principal can throw a football! The next few days all the kids were asking, 'When's my turn?'"

Play as a talking tool

Eileen, who works at Chesapeake City Elementary School in Chesapeake City, Maryland, often uses Play to help students with discipline problems. "If I can find a way for students to work out their anger first, it's easier to get them talking about what happened. So I ask what they like to do. For a lot of boys, it's football or baseball.

"So we'll go outside or to the gym, getting them out of the environment where they got in trouble. As we throw the ball back and forth, they unwind and usually what's bothering them—and what actually caused the behavior—comes out. I remember one boy had gotten into a fight," she continues. "As we played catch, he said his older brother was beating on him at home—to toughen him up. That's why he was so angry when he was at school. Once we knew the cause, we could help him.

"For me, Play is a way to connect with students. That's being there for them."

Toys in the office

Not every student likes sports, so Eileen keeps other toys in her office, such as miniature cars. "I dug into one boy's interests and found he likes to go fishing and crabbing. So I put together a folder of stuff he'd created about fishing to look at when he comes down for a timeout. Another boy came in and as we talked, we discovered that his dad and I bought a new lawn tractor on the same weekend. He thought that was cool. He has some behavior problems, so any connection I make helps us talk more easily about what's really going on and how he can make better choices."

The key, Eileen says, is that students understand that the office is a place where they can feel at home. Play helps encourage that.

"They don't just come by for getting in trouble," she says. "It's way more good than bad. Now they stop by to show me projects they've created. I have a positive relationship with most of the students."

"Students understand that the office is a place where they can feel at home."

"Who'm I Talkin' To?"

Rick Wagoner grew up without a father. "We lived in a small town in western Kentucky. My mother cut grass for a living," he says. "Our family lived on about $5,000 a year, though I never knew we were poor.

"I joined the band in seventh grade and I enjoyed playing the drums. But when I got to high school, the football coach wanted me on the team. I wanted to play drums too, but they told me I couldn't do both. So I told my mother, who's about 5'2", that I was quitting band for football."

This, to put it mildly, didn't fly.

"After I picked up my broken body next to the drum set she had just bought me," Rick jokes, "I decided to carry on with music. The director made me the drum line section leader, and I taught drummers throughout high school."

Near the end of high school, Rick's mentor — "the father figure in my life," he says — asked what he was going to study in college.

"The computer age was just starting and I enjoyed tinkering with computers. So I told this gentleman that it came down to computers vs.

"After I picked up my broken body …"

teaching music.

"He asked why I liked computers and I said, 'There's a lot of money to be made in computers.' He asked why I was considering music and I said, 'Because I love kids. I want to share my love of music with them.'

"This gentleman looked me in the eye: 'Seems like a simple choice. Do what makes you happy, because money sure won't buy it for you.'"

The richest man

Listening to his mentor, and now so thankful for his mother, Rick has found untold "wealth" as the director of the music department for Avon Schools, in Avon, Indiana.

He shares this wealth with his belief that music prepares children for life: "Because music touches the feelings, it can take you to the mountain-top and 30 seconds later you're in the valley, because it can be frustrating learning an instrument. It takes practice—just like I have to practice being a better daddy, a better husband, a better teacher. You learn to make those choices with an instrument."

With the increasing focus on test scores, however, Wagoner often hears the arts aren't important. "I call this feeling the 'big dog,'" he says. "That big ol' dog is attacking the fine arts and we have to fight that dog." Music is essential to education, he says, "because it first touches your heart and soul, then your mind. Most teachers try to educate the mind first, but it's the heart and soul where we find our motivation to learn, and there is no better way than the arts to ignite it."

That's why The FISH! Philosophy fits so well with the beliefs Rick has honed in nearly 20 years teaching music. "A lot of teachers will say fun is secondary in education. No, it's primary. You can't reach students without it," he says.

"The FISH! Philosophy," he continues, "is about awareness of our choices, being there for the group, and lifting each other's spirits. It's all about creating an atmosphere that's conducive to learning."

To foster this learning in each of his kids, whenever Rick has an important point to make to his band students at Avon Intermediate School, he says to the entire band: "Who am I talking to?" In unison, more than 50 voices shout back: "ME!"

"I work hard to show the kids that this program does not become theirs until they actually take control of it," he says. "My average class size is right around 55. I want to make sure they know they are important to the band program, and how important it is for each of them to be there.

"So I start with my first-chair flute player and I say, 'Rebecca, you're the most important person in the room. You've really got to be focused because without you we are nothing.' And I go to the second-chair flute player. 'Jennifer, you are the most important person in this room; without you we are nothing!' By the time I get around to six or seven kids, they're all laughing, 'cause they know what I'm doing."

"Rebecca, you're the most important person in the room."

Teaching responsibility

Along with this importance, Rick also gives his kids lots of responsibility. He acknowledges this can be risky.

"One summer I had a kid going into seventh grade—incredible tuba player named Jack. In summer band I had six beginning tuba players and I was stretched a little thin. So, for a week, he helped me out."

At the end of the week, during a lunch break, one of the staff came in to see Rick, hands on her hips, tapping her foot. "You need to keep an eye on these kids," she told Rick. "I just caught boys outside unsupervised. They were kicking a ball against the wall, and it got stuck in a vent!"

Rick apologized. "I'll take care of it."

"And another thing," the staff member said, "this one kid seemed to be the leader. I asked him who he was and he said he was the teacher!"

When Rick talked to the boys, he recalls, "It turned out Jack had said, 'Hey guys, we gotta learn this. If you really focus all week long, for the last 20 minutes of class we'll go outside and play wall ball.' He used the same kind of carrot system I used when I was a drum line section leader in high school.

"So they made a little mistake," Rick admits. "I looked at the kids and said, 'Oops, you messed up, didn't ya?' But they knew I still loved them. Lesson learned and we move on. Jack was trying to do the best he could for the other kids. What a great kid! How can I not love a kid like that?"

Rick adds, "It's always on the edge of being out of control around here. Controlled chaos, you could say. But it's important that we give up that control. Some teachers don't want to do that because they want to be in total control. But my experience has been that if you control kids like that, they're prisoners—and prisoners don't want to learn.

"Do they make mistakes? Don't we all? But here's the payoff: At Avon, when I ask the kids to jump, they don't just say, 'How high?' They say, 'Sure, Mr. Wagoner, I'll jump as high as you want, but can I also do a double back-gainer and a triple flip on the way down?' Man, I am so amazed by these kids. Give 'em some ownership, hold the bar high, and they just take off."

The real trophies

It wasn't always like this, Rick says. At one time in his career, he held the bar a bit too high—for himself.

"Every year our kids, along with about 180,000 others, go to the state music contest. The scores are published in a book that goes to all the band and choir directors. I could never understand why the kids were not getting a perfect score. I always took the judges' suggestions and worked so hard on that with the kids—you know, play softer here, more balance here—but I wanted that perfect score. We came close, but never all perfect with three judges. And I obsessed about it; I was gritting my teeth about it. Until one of my mentors said, 'Rick, you need to take your eyes off the perfect score and put it on the kids.' I stopped thinking about the plastic and wooden trophies and focused on the real trophies—our children. I started to look at every one of them as a gift from God; this was a big step in my spiritual journey as well."

It didn't happen overnight. Rick admits, "I went from yelling, screaming, kicking stands, and throwing my baton, to yelling, screaming, and throwing my baton. Then I went to just yelling and screaming, and instead of throwing my baton, I just started dropping it. The next step was looking at the band when we didn't play well, gritting my teeth, and saying, 'Amazing.' Whenever I say amazing, this is when I want to get mad because we're not paying attention ... Instead, I find one kid and I look in her or his eyes, and I remember what this is all about."

"... instead of throwing my baton, I just started dropping it."

Pushing each other back in the ring

Another tool Rick uses to keep himself on track is recalling his old days of teaching in the inner city of Indianapolis—until he was RIFed. "That's reduction in force," he laughs.

In his second year, he saw a little girl shot by an 11-year-old who was seeking revenge against someone else. It was tough and intense. "But," he says, "I loved those kids. Schoolwork was not their priority every day. Safety was. Just love them and they'd work so hard for you.

"The other thing I loved there is that when we walked into the staff room, all our professional differences were put aside. You'd sit down and say 'Jimmy was really upset in class. What's up with him today?' Another teacher would chime in, 'I heard Jimmy and Johnny are gonna get in a fight after school and Jimmy's afraid he might get shot.'

"So we'd all work at intervention together and it created a bond. A teacher might come in hanging his head after a tough morning, feeling like a total failure, and it was our job to pump him back up. It was almost like a boxing match where the boxer comes back to the corner and we're the manager, massaging the shoulders and pouring liquids, getting ready to push him back into the ring."

"It was almost like a boxing match."

For perspective, Rick compares his current school. "Sometimes we take each other for granted, especially in suburban schools. We forget how good we have it, and we get caught up in personality conflicts. Kids can see that. They understand when staff members love being around each other and when staff members don't. It's so important that they see that we love being around each other, that we are here for the same purpose—because if kids don't see that, how can they model what we are not modeling?"

Rick says teachers must also model their values and priorities. "I always keep pictures of my family and other important symbols on the front of my podium," he says. "This is me. I really try to bring my whole self to work. I tell them about my family. They know about my two girls. They hear the crazy stories like the one about the night wild dogs attacked our golden retriever at two in the morning, about how I run out to chase them away, arms swinging, and suddenly realize the floodlight's on and I'm standing in my backyard in my underwear."

It's this level of vulnerability that helps create his bonds with students, with teachers, with the entire school.

It's about them

When Rick interviews prospective teachers, the first question he asks is: "Why do you want to teach?"

"Every once in a while, they'll look at me and say, 'What other job gives you three months off in the summer?' If I get that, I close my book and the interview's over. Or I'll hear something like, 'I love the feeling I get when I teach music.' That's closer, but it's still about me.

"The answer I'm looking for—which I get about half the time—is, 'I want to teach because I love kids.'" It's these teachers that make the cut with Rick.

"With one word you can destroy a kid's spirit."

He says, "I tell all of my beginning teachers that teaching is incredibly dangerous. It's never any of the reasons they think. The reason teaching is so dangerous is that with one word you can destroy a kid's spirit. So we have to watch ourselves. Is what we are saying meant to truly help them and never to hurt them?

"I have kids who don't get hugged at home, who don't have anyone to tell them, 'You're a great kid. I'm proud of you,' give them high-fives; give them responsibility. But you should come to our band room. It's crazy. I've got six bands at the intermediate school, one class at the high school, and I'm in charge of 15 other directors. I'm constantly answering e-mail or on the phone and there's always kids standing around. I'll say, 'What do you need?' They'll say, 'Oh nothing.' 'So you're just hanging out?' 'Yup.' When kids just hang out in the band room because they feel at home, that's a good thing.

"See," he says, "if we take care of children and love them and help them become great people, everything else falls into place. I don't care about the trophies anymore, but I do care about the process. If we help our kids become good people first, we're gonna get great band students, great math students, great science students, and eventually good moms and dads.

"I tell kids," he says, "'We're here to learn about life. If we learn about band, that's great too.'"

We do not stop playing because we grow old, we grow old because we stop playing.

—Benjamin Franklin

The Cheerleader
and the Football Player

When Katrina Smith's students struggled with their Spanish tenses, she decided to "cheer" them up.

"By the time we get to the subjunctive tense, they've learned so many tenses that they get them confused," says Katrina, a teacher at Amelia High School in suburban Cincinnati.

"I was determined to help them remember, so one day, off the top of my head, I started telling this story about a cheerleader and a football player.

"It turns out the football player's name was Ron—which is part of the verb form used to create the subjunctive tense. And Ron wasn't any good for the cheerleader. He didn't treat her right; he was going out on her. As I'm telling this," she laughs, "I'm running around the room, drawing the kids into the story, and trying to figure out where I'm going with this thing.

"Now, the cheerleader's friends told her, 'You need to get rid of this guy.' Finally, she saw the light and said, 'You're right. I've had it. I'm gonna drop Ron!' That's what I was trying to help them remember: You have to drop the *ron* part of the verb before you add the other subjunctive endings. I scratched Ron off the chalkboard, and the kids are laughing and carrying on.

"Then I explained that the cheerleader's friends were so happy that they broke into—what else?—a cheer! It went like this: 'Ra (pronounced rah), ras, ra, ramos, ran!' Those are the verb endings you add to create the subjunctive tense, so I led the class through this chant in a sing-songy cheerleader voice, doing those little cheerleader jumps—well, I was trying to do them …" Katrina laughs.

"We chanted it over and over: 'Ra, ras, ra, ramos, ran! Ra, ras, ra, ramos, ran!' From that day on, whenever a subjunctive verb came up, all I had to do was say 'cheerleader,' and they knew what to do."

"They were so happy that they broke into—what else?—a cheer!"

Adding the spices

According to Smith, Play is an important part of her teaching—and that means being open to new ways of presenting material. "Students tell me that when they don't like a teacher, it's usually because, in their words, 'I don't understand it, and the teacher won't help me.' That's when the kids shut down with a teacher. My philosophy is you never quit. You keep trying until you find a way to get the information through to them. As long as kids see you're still trying, they'll be with you."

Smith says two Spanish teachers were her favorites in high school: "It was an adventure to go to class, not because it was scary, but because you never quite knew what to expect." That's why Smith tries to change activities every 10 to 15 minutes.

"My kids have so many different learning styles that we try to use a variety of strategies. I turn lessons into games and competitions. I have clear goals but it's the spices that go along with the drills, reading, and writing that make it more enjoyable. Getting shy, introverted students to speak in a foreign language class can be a monumental task, but it's easier when you get them in an interactive game, where everybody's having fun."

Smith admits that in order to make an impact, there's a limit to silliness. "I can't go so overboard that I lose the ones who want to be cool—even though inside they really like it. We have serious moments. We have funny moments. We have lively moments. It's a potpourri of emotions and hard work. And there may be times when some kids say, 'What's wrong with Señora Smith? She's crazy. What is she having us do now?' But"—she grins—"they'll come back a few years later and say, 'I remember when we did that skit where we dressed up, or the time you made up that wild story about the cheerleader. That was fun.'"

To me, recognition is just a teacher or someone saying, you know, "You're working, you're making progress and I'm proud of you."

—*Scott, junior*

CREATIVITY HAS NO ROUTINE

We all have routines. Routines offer familiarity and comfort. But learning something new often requires a bit of discomfort, kind of like the butterflies in your stomach just before you experience the thrill of going 70 miles an hour in a roller coaster.

Einstein went so far as to say that before an idea can be great, it must be absurd—outside what is safe and ordered. That's why some of the best ideas come at unexpected times: in the shower, grocery shopping, in the middle of the night. Play requires breaking routines in order to trigger new ways of looking at accepted concepts.

Here are a few questions to play around with: How willing are you to experiment with the routines in your classroom or school in order to make learning more fun and engaging? How might it keep students interested? How might it help keep you interested?

As Albert Einstein said, "Play is the greatest research."

Let's get to work.

The Book
Without an Ending

Students at Aiken Elementary School are writing a book without an ending.

"After our principal, Sharon Foret Cagle, introduced us to The FISH! Philosophy, the students decided to create a book of suggestions on how to apply these principles to their lives," explains Jana DeHart, who teaches gifted and talented fifth graders in Aiken, South Carolina.

"The book, called *Minnows Can FISH! Too*, has four sections, one for each of the principles. Since the kids created the book, each new class has added their own thoughts to it—and we will keep adding every year. The FISH! Philosophy never ends," she laughs, "so why should our book?"

A small sampling

Here's a sample of the students' suggestions—so far:

Be There

Make such great eye contact with your teacher that she thinks:

a) There's lipstick on her teeth.
b) She's having a bad hair day.
c) Her teaching is phenomenal.
d) All of the above.

Pretend that your science teacher is an alien. You must pay close attention to the scientific method she is demonstrating or risk being blasted into orbit to become an experiment on her planet.

Do the wave when anyone answers correctly.

Play

When given a writing assignment, pretend that your paper is a dragon and your pen is a sword. You must write to slay the dragon.

Join the Choo Choo Chat Birthday Train dance to the tune of "The Locomotion" even though you know it's just a hair shy of being dorky.

Make Their Day

Stand quietly in line even though the teacher may wonder what you are up to.

Buy ice cream at lunch for friends with your ice cream money.

When choosing teams at recess, shout to the new kid, "We need you!"

Choose Your Attitude

When riding to school early in the morning, pretend you are on the Starship Enterprise™ or headed to where "no man (or woman) has gone before."

As you prepare to take your math test, consider all the right answers as the numbers you need to win the state lottery.

When someone new joins you and your friends at recess, think, "The more the merrier!"

Working together to create a whole

In addition to writing their thoughts, Jana says, the Aiken Elementary students also photographed scenes and designed the book artistically. Their enthusiasm—and learning—was remarkable.

"They used graphics software to create each page. They learned technology, cooperation—they worked in teams—using writing, critical, and creative skills." But, Jana notes, they didn't stop there.

Through collaboration, teamwork, and FISH!, the class learned the biggest lesson of all. "They learned that they control their own attitudes," Jana says. "You can't beat that!"

"You Gave Us Back Our Child"

At Heritage Middle School in Middlebury, Indiana, when they say education pays, they mean it.

In the fall of 2003, four teachers launched a new corporation and "hired" their students.

"Too many of our students were not following through on their responsibilities—getting homework done, coming to school," says Michele Tibbs, an eighth grade science teacher. "We watched *FISH!* and saw how The FISH! Philosophy could help us look at our work in a new way. We decided to have some fun while we helped our students see school in a new way."

They called the pseudo-corporation BHTL, for Be Happy to Learn (it also stood for the first initials of the teachers' last names). Each subject area was renamed: Science became research and development, math became accounting, language arts became public relations, and social studies became human resources. Students who completed their work received a "paycheck" every two weeks. The check, complete with their name and the corporation logo, entitled them to participate in Fun Fridays.

"They called the pseudo-corporation BHTL, for Be Happy To Learn."

On Fun Fridays, for example, the science class merged fun and learning by designing balloon rockets and making things bubble and fizz. They built carriages that allowed eggs to survive high drops. Did they get to blow things up? "No," Michele laughs, "but that is the number one question asked of science teachers."

Fun Fridays also gave students the chance to practice The FISH! Philosophy. "The first Friday we made chocolate candy," Michele says. "Students got to keep half and the other half they gave away to staff members. It might be a person they hadn't gotten along too well with, or someone who was special to them. Either way, it made their day and strengthened relationships."

According to Michele, BHTL was a more positive way of approaching students than the staff had used in the past. "We didn't nag them nearly so much," she says. "It was their choice, and as in real life, each choice carried a clear consequence. If you didn't do your homework, you didn't participate in Fun Fridays."

Those students who missed out on Fun Fridays, however, received a hidden benefit. During that time, while they did homework, they received more one-on-one time with teachers.

"It gave us a chance to get to know the kids a little better, to figure out why they weren't fulfilling their responsibilities, and to try to find ways to help them succeed," Michele says "It also gave them extra time to make up their work for full credit. Kids started to understand that what they did at school really set the stage for what they were going to do later in life."

Being there for Reid

One of Michele's "employees" was a red-haired, freckle-faced eighth grader. His name was Reid.

"His seventh grade teachers told me he could never sit down and they weren't always sure where his sense of humor was coming from," Michele says. "He was in detention sometimes, and though his IQ placed him in the gifted and talented group, his grades didn't reflect it."

Michele thought back to her own school days. "My older sister never got a grade lower than an A- from kindergarten through high school. I was constantly compared to her and I was nothing like her. My teachers made me feel like I was less than I was. They didn't look for the person that I was."

Except for her science teacher, she says. "He never compared me to my sister. Sometimes all it took for him to make me feel special was to write a little note on my paper when I did well."

Like her role model, Michele decided not to judge Reid based on his past. On the first day of school, when he introduced himself, they found a connection right away.

"Hi," he said. "My name's Reid. That's R-e-i-d."

"Hey, I really like your name because that's my grandmother's maiden name," Michele said.

Reid's eyes widened. "And she spelled it just like me?"

"Yup. Maybe we're related ..." Reid laughed. Maybe this teacher, this year, was going to be different.

The conversation took just a few seconds, but it set a tone. Michele recalls, "He made me laugh that very first day. He was a comedian all right. I think the message had been, 'You have to behave in a certain way,' and that was the only way. We decided to go with him a bit and joked right back. We made it clear that it was okay to be the class clown as long as it's not keeping others from learning."

> "My teachers made me feel like I was less than I was."

A new hero

Michele could see that Reid was highly intelligent by the way he answered questions and by the way he asked them. "When he didn't finish his homework, we'd say, 'Reid, you're so smart, you already answered this question in class. Why not take a little time to write it down?'"

Michele says, "I don't know if there was one specific thing our team did that told Reid it was okay to do well. We all tried to be there for him. When we told him it was cool that he liked the blues instead of pop music, it made his day."

The approach worked. For outstanding achievements, BHTL designated students as Employee of the Month and "Reid was one of the first," Michele says. "We'd use that with him too, reminding him that 'Hey, you're a role model now for the class.'" And, on his first report card, Reid got all As and Bs.

"He was so proud," Michele says. "Before, his parents had punished him for his behavior in school. But this time he ran into class and said, 'My parents are taking me to dinner as a reward, and I get to choose where we're going!'

"Later that year Reid's mother told us, 'You made it cool for him to be smart. You made it okay for him to help his friends who were struggling. He used to be recognized for being the class clown, but you recognized him for being smart. You gave us back our child.'"

Restoring a sense of purpose

At the eighth grade graduation, Reid unexpectedly walked to the microphone and called Michele and her team to the front. "He had designed a logo for our corporation on his computer, transferred it onto T-shirts, and presented each of us with a T-shirt. The class also collected $100 to finance the corporation's activities next year!"

But that wasn't all Michele received.

"My teammates, my students, The FISH! Philosophy—they all gave me the sense of belonging and purpose I'd been missing. Early in my career I was idealistic about the world and what my classroom was going to be like," she says. Then the world got in the way—parents who didn't support education at home, overcrowded schools, lack of community support. "I became a follower and got drawn into negativity. When I saw the *FISH!* video, I was one of the first to say, 'This isn't going to work.'

"But then I realized, if my happiness depended on everything around me being perfect, I was never going to be in control of my life. The FISH! Philosophy reminded me that I could be the teacher I wanted to be. I could look at situations differently and choose to laugh about them. I didn't have to be in a rut. I could be creative and try new things.

"I credit my teammates for helping me get my idealism back," she says. "We had so much fun bouncing ideas off each other. They helped me find the person who was still inside of me, wanting to figure out how to have fun so kids want to learn."

We are most
nearly ourselves
when we achieve
the seriousness
of the child at play.

—*Heraclitus*

MAKE THEIR DAY

MAKE THEIR DAY

Make Their Day is often a big production at schools—from letter jackets to trophies to valedictorians. It's wonderful to recognize, and be recognized for, hard work and accomplishment. It's a natural, human motivator. It's what many students, and teachers, strive for every day. But what if you're not the best athlete, scholar, or musician? What if you're not the best, the brightest, or the boldest? You may get the message that something is only worth doing if it's rewarded. And if you're not rewarded, then perhaps what you're doing must not be important. To combat this, it's important to remember that even the simplest of actions can make all the difference. Remembering a student's name. Holding the door open for someone whose arms are full of books. Recognizing another person's opinion even if it differs from yours. Congratulating someone on his or her hard work, no matter how small the project. When we show others that they are worthy of our respect and concern, we set a tone for our school that invites *everyone* to feel included. We foster a sense of hope that encourages kids *and* adults to keep trying. We create an atmosphere of support and compassion.

Give to give Make Their Day means taking a genuine interest in the gifts of others. It does not come with strings attached. It is not designed to "get" something—for example, praising one child publicly so others will fall into line. Make Their Day is a heartfelt contribution intended for no other purpose than to bring a little joy into someone's life. But there is a side effect. You may find that when you make this effort— not because you want something but because that's the person you want to be—you receive an internal gift that gives purpose to your *own* life. Not only are you helping others, but also you're helping yourself. As educator David St. Germain says, "When you're there for someone, all of a sudden it can go to your heart and then it becomes make your moment, make your day, make your month, make your year, make your life."

A Universal Language

Piper Nichols, a second-grade public-school teacher in Rochester, Minnesota, *wondered* if her job was changing when three students told her that they were homeless, living in shelters. "One came to me in the middle of a Minnesota winter with no coat, boots, mittens, or backpack. I tried to find those things for her without offending her family."

She *suspected* her job was changing when a student told her she didn't like the music Piper was using. "She said she preferred the 'swear' music she listened to at home. She was six years old."

But Piper *knew* her job was changing when, after asking the class to settle down, a little boy called her a b___ch. "I was shocked. I stood there thinking my second-grade son doesn't even *know* that word," she says.

She began to have doubts about her profession. "I wasn't sure how much longer I could teach like this. We're not just teaching academics anymore. And there is nothing in our curriculum that makes time to connect with kids. It's expected that you'll figure it out along the way, but no one really teaches you how to do it."

She considered a discipline plan that exacted more punishment with each infraction. "I wanted the kids to know I was the boss and I was going to lay down the law. The discipline plan gave kids choices, but it seemed like the only choices were, 'Do exactly what I want or suffer the consequences.' It just didn't feel right for me."

One of Piper's friends, who taught at another school, had a different idea. "How about building a relationship with your students?" she asked Piper. "Instead of throwing out more rules for them to fight against, show them how *they* can change the classroom, not just *you*." She told Piper about The FISH! Philosophy.

"How about building a relationship with your students?"

A changing landscape

Though Piper was apprehensive about taking time to introduce the philosophy, she felt it was too important to ignore. "I had curriculum to get through and I was behind because the class was out of control. We kept up with our math and reading but for two weeks we talked about each of The FISH! Philosophy principles and practiced them with each other."

Emotional safety, she quickly learned, was a big concern for her students. "A lot of the issues we were having came out of kids feeling uncomfortable. Some schools in Rochester had a lot of socioeconomic and cultural diversity; others in the district were highly homogenous. We had just gone through a redistricting to make sure each school had an even rate of diversity, as well as enrollment. Many of our students were new and had to leave all their good friends behind."

In addition, several of her students needed interpreters. "It was hard to communicate," Piper says "Sometimes when I was talking, they'd just get up and wander around the room. When I indicated I wanted them to sit down and listen, they just looked at me and walked off. Of course, there were plenty of kids who spoke *English* who did the same thing."

With parents, Piper occasionally encountered even more differences. On a special occasion, Piper did face painting and brought candy for the class. "I learned later that the shell of the candy contained an ingredient that one cultural group is not allowed to eat," she says. "Some of the parents were upset, and when they got angry, their children were upset. I worked hard to choose my attitude. I listened, didn't get upset, really watched my body language, and, through our interpreter, helped them understand that I wasn't trying to offend anyone. I was actually trying to make their kids' day. Once they understood that, we grew to respect and understand each other."

Piper tells another story: "I love to use music in class, and to learn fire safety we sang a song with motions, which was better than just reading a book about it. One of the parents, for religious reasons, did not want their child to participate. So we talked and I very respectfully explained that the singing had nothing to do with religion but was part of our curriculum. If they didn't want their child to participate, that was okay, but I couldn't stop doing it for the others."

What was the result? "At our spring concert, we sang songs about what we had learned, and the child sang with us. I think it was because we had built trust. They saw that The FISH! Philosophy was not a religion. Instead, it's something that any culture or religion can take hold of. I'm very religious. I can't think of any religion in which these principles aren't a part."

"I wanted them to sit down and listen. They just looked at me and walked off."

Don't feel boxed in

Despite their varied backgrounds, Piper's students discovered they had something in common: They all brought worries with them to school from time to time.

"We began to share our concerns with each other, so we'd know we weren't alone. I told the class that my son, who'd had three open-heart surgeries, was very sick again. I told them, 'I'm very worried about my son, so I'm going to write my worry on this note, put it in a "worry" box and let it go during school.' They saw me modeling Choose Your Attitude and that became a big part of our classroom."

One day, a girl told Piper that her dog, whom she'd had since birth, was going to be put to sleep after school. "We wrote down her worry and put it in the box. She told me that while she was scared and sad, she was going to concentrate on school, then Be There for her beloved friend after school. Near the end of the day, I asked her to share her story and her choice with the class. The kids really worked hard to take care of her the rest of the day."

Earning recognition

While Piper had been reticent to take time for FISH!, she says, "When all was done, I got through the curriculum well before year's end. I had never finished all 12 units in math and this year I did. It was because of all the positive energy flowing and kids taking ownership. Instead of being recognized for being defiant, they wanted to be recognized for choosing their attitudes and making someone's day."

"I got through the curriculum well before the year's end."

The boy who had called Piper a name also made progress. "I asked him to tell me about his family and he started to open up. He's been tagged as the 'naughty kid' for so long that it takes time to break through. He knew I was trying to be fair and get to know who he really is. Toward the end of the year he made some poor choices again but I believe that it was fear of the unknown: 'Who's going to be my teacher next year? What am I going to do this summer? Will anyone be home with me?'

"I told him how proud I was of the *good* choices he had made and reminded him that he could still make those choices, even when he wasn't in my class. I told him I still cared about him and that I know the third grade teachers. I'm excited because I know they will care for him too."

Like her class, Piper earned recognition as well. "One of the best compliments my husband ever gave me came when he said, 'Honey, you're really into this FISH! Philosophy.' I thought, 'Hmm, where is he going with this?' But he went on to say, 'I appreciate how you come home and work so hard to Be There for our kids and not be consumed by what happens at school.'

"We've had a lot of ups and downs with our son who has the heart problems. Every day is a gift. I can't control how long this little guy is going to be with us, but I *can* control the love and joy we share and our time together, so when I lay my head down at night I won't think, 'Oh, I wish I had done that today.'"

Saying good-bye

As Piper said good-bye to her students on the last day of school, she cried. Her husband was there and said, "Dear, I don't understand. You wanted school to end so you could enjoy your summer. Can you explain it to me?"

As her kids ran toward summer, Piper responded, "It's because I was finally able to connect with these children. They let me into their hearts and souls, and I let them into mine. I said good-bye knowing I gave them my best."

A little kindness
from person to person
is better than
a vast love
for all humankind.

—Richard Dehmel

 **THOUGHT**

WHAT'S YOUR FOCUS?

If you want to change the world, first you have to change yourself.

That's what the fishmongers did in the *FISH!* video. When they focused on the physical discomforts of their work, they disliked it. When they focused on the attitudes they brought to their work, their environment suddenly became joyful, happy, and alive. The work itself never changed, only their view of themselves.

If you focus on how others frustrate, impede, or judge you, you are likely to feel angry, defensive, or resigned. But if you focus on how *you* may frustrate, impede, or judge others, instead of putting all your energies into trying to change them, they will suddenly seem different.

Looking at yourself first isn't usually an easy choice—but it *is* a choice. And it can change the whole world around you.

"If You Can't Say Something Nice …"

One of the rules in Charla Waxman's family was, *If you can't say something nice, don't say anything at all.*

"There was a girl in our high school," Charla says. "She was the kid that everybody made fun of. My friends mimicked her, even knocked books out of her hands. I never did those things—but I never told anyone to stop, either."

Charla, now a gang intervention consultant, recalls how one day she was waiting in the principal's office. "I was kind of a goody-goody, so I don't think I was in trouble, but they had a huge glass window and everybody could see who was there. So I'm sitting there, and this same girl walks in."

Charla squirmed, thinking, "If she sits next to me, somebody's going to see and my friends are gonna tease me unmercifully!" Sure enough, the girl sat next to her. Charla started to panic. "What if she talks to me? If anyone sees her lips moving and I'm the only one here, I'm gonna get razzed so bad."

The girl turned to Charla and smiled. "Oh, you're Charla, right? I always thought you were nice and I always thought you were pretty."

Charla felt about an inch tall. "Without knowing it, she told me who I was at that moment, and it was an ugly revelation. I'd been in probably a dozen classes with her and I realized I'd never heard her speak. Second, for her to say I was nice and I was pretty—in my mind I was neither one of those things at that moment. I'd been hiding behind the cool kids and the popular kids … I was a fake.

"In that moment," Charla recalls, "she taught me more than even my teachers did. From that point on, I don't think I ever hesitated to tell my friends to stop when they made fun of people.

"Now, when I talk with high school students, I tell them that story. Because the kids who retreat the most are the ones we need to Be There for, to Make Their Day. Each of us has to choose if we want to be a person who's going to do those things for others."

"… it was an ugly revelation."

The Unreadable Assignment

To create a more effective learning environment, Jason Pelowski gives his students an assignment they can't read.

"I have a slight learning disability—dyslexia," says Jason, who teaches math and video production at Chaska High School in suburban Minneapolis. "In almost every class I hear kids use the word *retard*. '*Oh, I'm such a retard.*' '*That's so retarded.*' As soon as that word is used, it shuts down the learning environment for students in class who've been working hard to overcome their learning disabilities, and suddenly they're back 10 steps.

"So I give students an assignment to help them understand what it feels like to be in that spot. All they know is that it's an article on camera angles. They don't know that several students will get articles that are missing some words. They have five minutes to read the article, then take a short test where they find six words.

"Everybody gets the first word, no problem. The second word, the doctored articles don't have it, and you start to see some frustrated looks. By the third word, the kids are saying, 'What's going on here?' I say, 'I gave you the directions. Didn't you understand?' 'Yeah.' 'What's the problem?' By the last word, they're really upset—and I always make sure that the last word is 'ineffective.'

"I ask people to raise their hands who felt they were *ineffective* taking this test. They've just had a small taste of what it's like to try to learn with a learning disability."

Jason says it's important that he establish a safe environment in his classroom—physically, verbally, and emotionally. "I could just tell them not to say certain words, but it's more effective if they see it for themselves. I'm not trying to force my beliefs on them. I'm trying to help them see that their words have an impact on others.

"What happens is that the use of the word *retard*, as well as other hurtful words, diminishes very quickly. Somebody will blurt it out and instantly say, 'Sorry, anyone who was offended, sorry. I'm working on it.' Just to know they are trying makes such a difference. In the process I see a ton of cliques break down. I see the student dressed in all black working with the kid in sports, and they didn't even know each other before. They may find out they have some things in common—they're fun to hang around with, different from their other friends. They may gain some new outlooks. That's a FISH! classroom."

Choosing success

When Jason first saw the *FISH!* video, he thought, " *This is a business thing. How's it going to work for* me?' I just didn't grasp it right away." But David St. Germain, Chaska's professional development coordinator, helped him see how FISH! connected to his goals. "The four statements took a cloudy image and made it clear to me the kind of classroom I wanted."

He learned a new way of being there for his students. "My first year I thought I knew it all, and found out quickly I did not. Students would push my buttons, trying to get a reaction—and they'd get it. I'd go home and worry, 'Did I handle that situation right?'"

But now, he joins forces with his students, inviting them to help set mutual expectations. "The students get a chance to tell me what they think their role is and what my role is," Jason says. "In the process, we see that a lot of things—such as respect or accountability—are everybody's role. It's not just their responsibility to listen; it's also mine. It's not just their responsibility to learn; I'm a learner too.

"If I see that students aren't doing what they agreed was their responsibility, we'll have a conversation about it. I'll say, 'The first day of class I asked everybody, *Who wants to be successful? Who wants me to be successful?* Everyone raised their hands. My concern here is I'm seeing things that in my experience have led to unsuccessful results.'

"When I approach students in these situations, I'll see their faces scrunch up a bit, because they're ready for me to lay into them. But if I choose my attitude and calmly ask questions that help them think through what happened, and what they'd like to have happen next time, they open up, and think, 'That wasn't so bad. Maybe Mr. Pelowski isn't just here to lay into me. Maybe he's trying to help me learn.'

"Now, if they take it as, 'That wasn't so bad. I got away with that one,' we're probably going to have another conversation. I'm not going to get angry about it but there *is* a natural consequence—and it's that they may *not* be successful."

In such cases, realizing they have the choice is the lesson. "A group of students was putting together a video to promote homecoming, and they were joking about having a short clip in which a male student asks another male student to the dance. As we talked, and I asked questions, they finally moved down the path of realizing, 'Wait a minute. Gay and lesbian students are part of our school. Is this piece going to make them feel unsafe? Yes, and that's not right.' They didn't use the piece. I could have just said 'You can't

"There is a natural consequence and it's that they may *not* be successful."

do it'—and, if necessary, I would have—but they figured it out on their own and made a decision that kept it safe for our entire school community.

"When students are given the opportunity to really think through those kinds of issues, it boosts their self-confidence in life, and directly in the classroom. They see how much their choices impact others and shape their own success. I see kids start to take on a leadership role in class and start doing amazing things."

"How did you do that?"

When the classroom feels safe, Play flourishes. "I start with a tutorial, but after that, the concept of Play takes over," Jason says. "The students learn the technology by actually *playing* with it, putting together some goofy things. All of a sudden a student discovers something cool, and the whole class is huddled together in the edit suite, having fun, asking questions, becoming more curious and excited to learn."

In such an environment, Jason explains, everyone is a learner. "I always tell students at the beginning of the quarter that I'm not your teacher — at least not the way they usually think of a teacher as an authority figure who knows it all. I am a facilitator of their learning. I'm here to guide and support.

"When students ask me questions, I may direct them to other students who have asked that same question before or who have shown me how to do it. They realize I'm not the only resource in the classroom. Eventually, as they gain the confidence to try new things on their own, they become resources too, and the whole class is learning from each other."

As Play is critical to learning, Jason says, so is choosing your attitude. "Any creative work requires that we be able to accept criticism, to hear suggestions and input, look past our biases and filters, understand that others may have a different opinion. Plus, when you work with technology, things don't always work the way we want, so we continually choose to adjust and make the best of a bad situation."

A big part of learning is being willing to accept input, then make your own decisions about what works. "I'll say, 'I'm not telling you that you have to change your piece. I'm just giving suggestions.' That's a big barrier for a lot of kids, because they think anything the teacher suggests, they have to do it that way. But that's not really learning. Of course, if I get a little over-bearing," he laughs, "students will say, 'Mr. Pelowski, Choose Your Attitude. You're not the grader right now. I just want some technical advice for now.'"

And when Make Their Day is part of the classroom environment, sometimes everyone is inspired. "One day, a student who was very technically adept complimented two other students. He told the entire class their work was amazing and that it raised the bar for everyone. These two students weren't viewed as so *technically* great, but were excellent storytellers.

"From that day on, I heard more students saying, 'I thought what you did here was great.' Or 'That was cool. How did you do that?' That's an empowering question to hear. You may have thought what you did was no big deal, but suddenly someone wants to know, 'How did you do that?' That's when real learning occurs, when the barriers between students come down."

"We continually choose to adjust ..."

"I need him"

At the beginning of each semester Jason has students fill out a sheet telling a bit about their interests, activities, and goals for the course. "That's where we start," he says. "Then I share some things about me, even funny stuff that happened to *me* in school. I try to get a few minutes of one-on-one time with students each week that goes beyond what we're studying. My goal is to learn something about a student that will make them feel safe and comfortable in my classroom. So I try to reach out to them, because they're not going to reach back until I do."

A few years ago, Jason explains, he decided to reach out to a student who had tried to commit suicide. "He was having a lot of trouble with drugs and alcohol and he left school to enter treatment for depression."

Jason called the boy's parents. "I told them, 'I need him. I realize he's not going to be in school, but if possible, he can still be part of our news program during first block.' When I talked to the student, I said, 'I don't want you to lose your connection with us.' He came to class everyday, for one block a day, to help us put out *Jump Start*, the high school's daily news program. He felt valued and he felt worth. And he had a lot of technical knowledge so his classmates asked him a lot of questions about how to do things.

"Many of the kids didn't know what had happened. But our class was safe enough that he was able to share what he was going through. He had good days and tough days. His classmates helped him through the year. He turned his life around, went on to college, and continued studying video production. He also began working with youth in treatment."

At the end of the year, the boy's mother wrote to Jason:

It is often said that just one teacher can make a memorable impact on a student's life. I want you to know that you have done just that for our son ...

Your encouragement and affirmation of his work empowered him at a time when his self-confidence was at its lowest. In the fourth quarter when he could barely handle being at school, you called and told him that you needed him ... I cannot tell you how powerful that was for him. By reaching out to him, you made it possible for him to feel good about being back at school .... It is in times like these when a good teacher becomes a great one. For our son, you have been not only a great teacher, you have been an example, supporter, mentor, and friend.

At the student's graduation party, Jason told him, "You're my hero."

"How's that?" the boy shrugged. "I'm just going to AA."

"You're not just going to AA," Jason said. "You're doing something that a lot of people in this world won't. You're taking responsibility for your life."

And that, Jason says, is what it's all about.

"When my students get compliments, when they're fulfilled by the work they're doing, I'm satisfied. I also get tremendous satisfaction from the positive choices they make in their lives … FISH! frames those choices so clearly."

 **THOUGHT**

FEAR GETS AN F

Any teacher who has proposed a new strategy in a faculty meeting only to have it ripped to shreds by others—or who has seen this happen to someone else—can understand the impact of a fearful classroom.

It's difficult to relax and learn in an environment where there is fear of being harassed for the way you look or think, fear of being made fun of, fear of making mistakes. In such situations, whether you are a student or teacher, you will probably stop taking chances and retreat to the safety of anonymity, conformity, or apathy.

According to psychologist Abraham Maslow, lower-level needs such as psychological safety must be met before humans can focus on higher-level needs like self-actualization—the desire to learn, grow, and become everything they can be. Noted researcher Alfie Kohn says students must be "comfortable before they can venture into the realm of discomfort" that learning requires.

Gauging safety

Consistency is a big test of an educator's commitment to emotional safety. Each of us tends to identify with, even admire, certain types of kids; perhaps they share our view of the world or remind us of what we were like at their age. Without being aware of it, we may greet them more enthusiastically or offer them more encouragement than we do others. We might, from time to time, even let them get away with comments we wouldn't accept from others. It's subconscious, but nonetheless sends a clear message to all our students: *We have two sets of rules, one for the kids we connect with and one for those we don't.*

Ensuring that a classroom is safe isn't just about imposing rules. Ironically, some teachers who crack down on behaviors that interfere with the lesson plan allow other behaviors — off-putting jokes, sarcasm, putdowns—that impede learning even more.

A study by students in one high school found the students heard an average of 25 anti-gay epithets per day and teachers who heard them failed to respond 97 percent of the time. We wouldn't stand by when a student's body is being pummeled; why do so when his or her spirit is?

That class was a lot of fun. And not like we just sat around and had fun ... we had fun while we learned stuff and we had fun in discussions. You didn't have to feel dumb about saying anything stupid because everyone was there to help you and not hurt you.

—Bell, *senior*

Turn It Up a Notch

At Avon Intermediate School, there's room at the table for everybody.

"Recently I bought furniture for the staff dining room—four tables with four chairs for each table," says principal Scott Raftery. "The next day, when I came in the dining room, the teachers had pushed all the tables together to create one huge table so they could eat like a big family."

The idea of "family" in the workplace is often an overused cliché, but it's a feeling Scott wanted to build when he introduced FISH! to Avon Intermediate, located in the suburbs of Indianapolis, Indiana.

"We're very professional here, but also personal," he says. "When you isolate yourself behind closed doors and don't get to know the people you work with, you miss out. A lot of us share with each other what's going on outside of school, our families, the ups *and* the downs. We listen and support each other and out of that, trust grows.

"It makes a difference. Say you bring a bit of baggage from home into a building where it feels like a second family, you know that this is a

"They created one huge table so they could eat like a big family."

place you can come to turn that feeling around."

Which in turn benefits the students. "It's a simple formula: A happy teacher is a better teacher. When they enjoy coming to work, being here eight to ten hours a day, that's definitely the kind of teacher I want working with my child."

An invitation

When Scott learned about The FISH! Philosophy, he immediately thought, *'That's us!'*

"When I saw the video," he says, "it reflected how our teachers take care of their 'customers'— our students and parents. I was sure FISH! could help us turn it up a notch." But first Scott had to assure his staff that FISH! wouldn't add any more to their plates.

"We're housing 1,050 students in one building, plus ten lovely portables—excuse me, *cottages*—that hold 750. Keeping up with the testing is intense. Teachers want to know that FISH! is not something that will require more work from them.

"I approached it like an invitation, like I was asking the entire staff out to dinner: 'Would you like to try this? Is this something extra that's going to take time away from kids and colleagues, or is it something we can do *while* we work with students and each other?' They liked that I wasn't demanding: 'We *will* be FISHY!'"

How many things are going right?

The Avon staff responded wholeheartedly and began by catching each other making someone's say. "We have forms by the mailboxes," Scott says. "If a colleague makes your day or somebody else's, you fill out the form, tell what the person did, and drop it in a box. Then I collect the nomination forms and list them in the staff bulletin every week or two to let the staff know what a wonderful job they're doing. In the last bulletin, there were seven and a half pages of Make Their Day moments.

"It's just people patting each other on the back—listening, giving someone a smile when they need it, bringing them coffee during a long meeting, helping with a lesson plan, covering a class. It reminds us how many things are going right, not just wrong."

Scott also created Make Their Day postcards to be mailed. "It only takes a second to fill one out. You wouldn't believe the people who say to me, 'I got a card from so-and-so. It happened to land in my mailbox on a Saturday when things weren't going so well, and it completely changed how I felt that weekend with my family.'"

The staff took this inspiration and found a way for the students to recognize each other. "A teacher had this ugly stuffed fish, so we created the traveling FISH! trophy," Scott says. "Classes nominate each other for the award, and you can't nominate yourself. Each week several classes are nominated, we draw names, and the winning class gets a box of fishy crackers and the coveted traveling trophy for a week. It's hilarious. When we announce the winning class over the intercom, you can hear the screams down the hall. The class also receives a journal that travels with the trophy. Students write in the journal about FISH! behaviors they observe during the week in the class. The activity also fulfills one of our academic goals of writing across the curriculum."

"It's just people patting each other on the back."

Inevitable phone calls

External activities like the Make Their Day forms and postcards have led to internal changes. "I think teachers try to Be There for their kids more," Scott says. "Teachers have received e-mails from parents saying how important it was to their children that they put their work aside and just took a few minutes to listen when the child needed them.

"You never know," he continues, "you could be the mother or father or counselor because the kid may not have that at home. Sometimes you just have to say, despite all the demands swirling around you, 'What's going on in my life right now is not as important as this child in front me.'"

And there are the inevitable phone calls from upset parents. "We all get them," Scott says. "In every case, the first couple of lines that come out of your mouth will probably set the tone for how that conversation is going to go. So you get to choose how you're going to react, and whether it will help or hurt that relationship."

As these choices have infused the school over the last few years, Scott says, the staff has come together as never before. "When the day's over, the bell has rung, and students are on the bus, you see this group of fifth grade teachers in the hallway, all standing around laughing and high-fiving and giving each other props. I saw one of them doing a cartwheel! Two years ago you'd maybe see a couple of teachers talking quietly. Now you see this big group, all together, saying, 'Whew, we got through another day.'"

When the staff is united, he says, it sends a powerful message to the kids: "Our students know expectations are going to be the same—whether you're in another classroom, the lunch room, or the halls," Scott says. "It's like when I was a kid and the neighbors called your folks if they saw you doing something that wasn't right."

Being FISH!

As principal, Scott must model the very behavior he seeks in his teachers and students. In any school, he explains, calmness starts at the top. "If I don't treat the people I work with right—if I'm not modeling FISH!— it's a joke. When teachers stop me in the hall and want to talk for 30 seconds, if I'm not being there for them even though I've got other places to be, they're gonna know, 'This is a bunch of bunk. This guy's not FISH!'

"Sure it's tough not to let stress get to you. But my job is not to unload on other people just because *I'm* stressed out. That's the worst thing I can do. Like they say, 'Don't let 'em see you sweat.' So that drive home from work? That's when I throw my luggage out on the highway."

He goes on: "I'm aware that what I say, what I do, how I act, how I listen, and my body language are out in front of me more than ever before in my educational life. It's my job to be a cheerleader, to show my human side, to make it a safe place where staff can take risks and try new ideas that can help kids. And if those ideas fail, it's not my job to yell, 'What the heck happened?' but rather, 'Hey, thanks for trying. What did we learn? What can we do better next time?'"

It's these caring, respectful relationships that carry the staff through: "Last week, we had a major computer glitch where we didn't think we'd be able to produce our report cards in time for parent-teacher conferences. Not too many people knew that behind the curtains we were frantic. A bunch of folks came together and stayed late to make it work. That's why last week was a great week. I suppose we could have had full meltdowns and torn each other's heads off. But because of the relationships we've developed here, that wasn't going to happen. The FISH! Philosophy has brought a kind of calm to Problem Solving 101.

"It's like in the book *All I Ever Need to Know I Learned in Kindergarten*," Scott says, "Robert Fulghum talks about holding hands and sticking together. That's being there."

> "My job is not to unload on other people just because *I'm* stressed out."

Ask the staff

At the end of every school year, Scott sends a "grade the principal" survey to every member of his staff. "It consists of 20-plus questions," he says. "The questions basically come down to, *What should I do more of? What should I do less of? What do I need to continue?*

"It's totally anonymous. I encourage them to use their left hand, color with crayon, whatever they want to do in order to throw me off," he adds, laughing. "The feedback form is a way for me to become a better person, personally and professionally. The only way I know if I'm doing the right thing is to ask the staff. I may think something's going well and is best for kids but if 90 percent of the staff says, 'Have you thought about this and this?' I'm definitely going to rethink it."

"Feedback is the *breakfast of champions*.®"

The survey also lets every staff member know her or his opinion counts. "Everybody on staff needs to be heard from, like the 10 teachers in the portables who I don't get out to see as much as I'd like. Or the paraprofessional who doesn't think her voice counts as much as the teacher she's working with when it comes to sharing her opinion."

Scott compiles all the answers and then gives it back to the teachers, "so they can see for themselves how the entire building feels about each question," he adds. "That's how I become a better principal. They say feedback is the *breakfast of champions*.®"

Scott also used his survey to see how FISH! was doing after its first year at Avon. "I wanted to see how it was going: 'Am I doing too much? Are they gagging on it?' As with any survey, I look for consensus and 90 percent were saying, 'This is awesome. It's so simple. It's made an impact.' I read comments like, 'I'm much more aware now of the impact I have on others,' or 'I think before I just blurt out something negative.'

"It shows that FISH! is in their consciousness now," he continues. "I used to be a counselor and it's called self-actualization. When you start seeing yourself and adjusting your own behavior, that's when you're making progress in becoming a better person—in my case, a better dad, husband, colleague, boss, son, brother. It's changed a lot of us and there's no turning back."

BREAKFAST OF CHAMPIONS® is a registered trademark of General Mills and is used with permission.

 **THOUGHT**

FIRST, LIVE IT

Researchers have found that when teachers attend workshops where the facilitators model attentiveness and caring, they are more likely to bring those same behaviors back to their classrooms. In other words, these attitudes are not simply learned; they are "caught."

Children rarely decide to adopt values on the basis of intellectual decisions. Instead, they absorb values through a kind of caring osmosis, by being around adults whose actions prove the truth of their commitments. Apply The FISH! Philosophy to your life first, and watch others around you catch it.

CHOOSE YOUR
ATTITUDE™

CHOOSE YOUR
ATTITUDE

CHOOSE YOUR ATTITUDE

It's easy to justify our attitudes by blaming something or someone else — to believe that external events, such as unpleasant experiences or people, are responsible for our reactions: *He made me upset! She didn't give me a choice!* As an educator you see this all the time in the classroom … and in faculty meetings … and in the staff lounge. ✒ While external factors may *trigger* our attitudes, we're the ones who decide — consciously or not — to express them. And these choices affect others. Just as happiness is contagious, negative attitudes also pass from person to person. If you doubt this, just try spending a day with a pessimistic or cynical person. Whoopie.

Choosing to change So how do we become effective "choosers"? To start, it helps to know where attitudes come from. ✒ Often without even being aware of them, attitudes are views we hold in response to situations or stimuli. Emotions are symptoms of attitudes and can lead us to what we are thinking underneath. Attitudes and emotions work together simultaneously and can be difficult to disengage. But not impossible. ✒ When we find ourselves in the middle of heated or frustrating situations in which we've reacted a certain way hundreds or even thousands of times, we will most likely continue a habit. That is, unless we are *aware* of our ingrained reactions and have practiced new responses to take their place. ✄ It helps to think ahead and to examine what you believe to be true. Is the person who is upsetting me really doing it intentionally? Do my reactions help solve the problem? Some think it's healthy to blow off steam when they feel they need to. But there is evidence that unloading your anger, without questioning why you're doing it, simply makes you angrier in the short term and reinforces a hostile habit. ✄ It helps to look at the language we use. Have you ever said or heard someone say: "Oh no, I have *that* kid next year!" "Only nine more months until summer vacation!" or "Why did I ever decide to become a *teacher?!*" Such statements tend not to fuel passion for one's *chosen* profession.

Power to choose People often use the phrase "Choose Your Attitude" when they really mean "choose the *right* attitude—or else!" But life ain't all sunshine and roses; sometimes angry or sad are what's called for. That's why Choose Your Attitude, at its core, is not about putting on a "happy face" or giving in to pressure to adopt the outlook that's "officially" acceptable. ✄ Choose Your Attitude asks only that you own *your choice* and not try to pass it off on something or someone else.

Once you accept that you are the only person who is choosing your attitude right now, you can decide whether to keep it or shape it into an attitude that's more satisfying. *You* control your attitude, not the other way around. ✒ Getting in a bad mood requires finding good reasons for *why* you're entitled to feel that way. Getting in a good mood requires the same effort.

The "Annihilation" Philosophy

A few years ago, when principal John DeFelice asked his staff at Boundary Street Elementary School to write the names of their three hardest-to-handle students—kids they wouldn't mind *not* having in their rooms—the ink practically jumped onto the paper. Then he asked the teachers to flip over their page and list three *positive* qualities about each child.

"Man, it was a hoot," says DeFelice, who now works at Pine Tree Hill Elementary School in Kershaw County School District, Camden, South Carolina. "Teachers sat there scratching their heads. Some would say things like, 'Well … he likes to *eat?*' I said, 'Good! We'll start with that. We'll tell him how wonderful he is for being a good eater!'"

Back then, DeFelice recalls, it wasn't easy being positive at Boundary Street Elementary, a pre-kindergarten through grade three school in Newberry, South Carolina. "The school is in a high-poverty area, with all the problems that come with it," DeFelice explains. "A high percent of students came to us academically below grade level. Shortly after I arrived, several teachers told me discipline was a big problem—they couldn't teach because the kids were out of control."

The first changes were external. "The physical appearance looked cluttered, so we cleaned it up," DeFelice says. Students built a goldfish pond in the courtyard. Trees and plants were brought in. Rooms were painted sage green and yellow, a big improvement from what DeFelice affectionately describes as "ugly gray."

The internal changes, he admits, took longer. "Teachers who choose to work in high-poverty schools usually have a very strong mission mentality," DeFelice says. "That was certainly true of this staff. They were working hard, but they were exhausted and disheartened."

Then, midway through his second year at the school, and more than a few paint brushes into his plan, DeFelice read a book called *FISH!* "I felt like I could have written this, but somebody just beat me to it," he laughs. "It wasn't a strategy about how to teach reading or math, it was a story about living to the fullest. It gave a name to what I'd been trying to accomplish. It let me know others felt the same way and gave me hope to keep trying."

> "They were working hard, but they were exhausted and disheartened."

That next Monday, DeFelice brought copies for the entire staff. "I told them, 'If you read this book, I will give you a half-day off and I will cover your class or find somebody to cover it.' Well," he says with a grin, "they were all over that offer."

Next, DeFelice put a large poster board in the faculty lounge and asked the staff to share their thoughts about the book—and how they could live The FISH! Philosophy in their school. "The overwhelming consensus was that we want to have a positive school, we want to have fun, and we can do it," he says. "It came down to 'We might not have all the resources other schools have, but we *are* going to be the most loving and nurturing.'"

A new philosophy

Inspiring his staff, FISH! also moved DeFelice to choose an entirely new attitude—one that challenged *years* of conditioning.

"I'm a happy guy, easygoing, and I love to play and joke with students," he says. "But I grew up in a strict home. My father was the kind of guy who when he said, 'Jump!' you asked, 'How high?'—on the way up. I carried that into my career as a teacher and principal.

"It was what I call the Annihilation Philosophy: *If you think you're going to act out or disobey me, I'm gonna annihilate you. I will humiliate, yell, scream, punish, take away recess, call your parents. I am more powerful than you and I will break you—to the point where you won't want to disobey me again.*

"I really thought I was doing kids a favor. I thought if I could just break 'em into submission, I could just open their heads up and pour in the information. But it had the opposite effect. They'd obey out of fear, but they didn't really want to learn because there was no love in it. I wasn't being there for them, I wasn't choosing the attitude I wanted, and it *sure* wasn't making anybody's day!

"So we talked about it and said let's start flooding these kids with positive attitudes and caring and kindness. Let's brag—not artificially—about every positive step they make."

"I am more powerful than you and I will break you."

New strategies

Talking about changing, of course, is easier than doing it. "If you ask any of us, 'Do you love kids? Do you come to work for kids?' we all have the right answers," DeFelice says. "The hard part is when little Johnny is being a horse's behind, yelling, or acting up. Suddenly your emotions take over and you blow up. So we needed to challenge and check each other to see if we're actually doing what we say we believe."

DeFelice began quietly listening to exchanges between teachers and kids. He brought these comments, anonymously, to faculty meetings. DeFelice always started with himself. "I'd say 'Let me tell you how I blew it today. At lunch a little girl wasn't getting in line. I said, 'Susie, what's your problem? You're not listening! Get in line!' As soon as I said it, I thought, *'Why did I do that?'*

"Then I asked the teachers, 'How could I have handled that in a more positive, building-up way versus annihilating that kid?' We'd talk about alternative strategies, then put them into practice."

Sharing such stories became a regular feature at staff meetings. "One day I heard a teacher tell a kid, 'I'm gonna watch you go to the water fountain 'cause I can't trust you.' The teacher just wants the child to hurry, but what does the child hear? *You're not trustworthy. You're bad.* After we talked about it, I heard the teacher say, 'Hey, you're fast! I'll bet you can go to the water fountain and back in 30 seconds. Matter of fact, I'm going to watch you to see how well you do that.' Same situation but the kid hears a completely different message."

In this process of choosing new attitudes, the staff also learned to Be There for each other—even when it felt uncomfortable. "It's easy for us to critique kids. That's what we're trained to do," DeFelice says. "What's difficult to do, and humbling, is for us to coach *each other*. A lot of times the recipient of the coaching is gonna swallow hard at first, but almost always, they'd come back and be thankful you cared enough to tell them."

He shares an example. "One day, I was really upset with a kid, and a teacher said to me, 'You're too angry to deal with this right now. I'll take care of it.' That wasn't easy to hear, but that's being a true friend."

Breaking through the wall

Unchecked, however, these instances of frustration lead to kids being sent to his office—90 percent of whom are furious because, DeFelice says, they feel the teacher unfairly picked on them.

"They weren't the only kid talking, they weren't the only kid out of their seat, they weren't the only one throwing paper balls. And you know what? A lot of times they're right. Teachers have a certain boiling point and they'll put up with talk, talk, talk, talk, and BAM! All of sudden they've had it and little Johnny just happened to be in the wrong place at the wrong time.

"So when a kid comes in and he's really mad, the first thing I do is to try to penetrate that anger to the kid's heart. I look in his eyes—and I'm talking to the point of being uncomfortable, maybe 30 seconds—and I really choose my attitude and look with compassion. And the first thing I say is, 'I love you.'

"Now you think that doesn't sound hokey? Of course it does. But I *do* love these kids and I can say it because they know I mean it. I couldn't say it if they didn't always see me in the halls, giving high fives and hugs, telling them how wonderful they are, eating lunch with them, joking around with them, popping into class, bragging on their progress, telling them, 'I hope I'm as cool as you are when I grow up.' I believe in them and that gives them hope—and that's love.

"So by being there and choosing my attitude, when I say 'I love you,' the defenses start to come down. I have a checklist of questions that help me and the kid to stay rooted in the positive. I'll say, 'Brian, what do you like to do best? What are you good at? What are some of the nice things your teacher has done for you?'

"If the teacher's with me, she may be furious, too, so hearing Brian helps bring her emotions down. Then I ask *her* to tell me something good about Brian. After she does, I turn to Brian and say, 'Did you hear what she said? It sounds like she cares about you. So, Brian, let me ask you a question: What do you think happened that made your teacher so frustrated? How do you think she feels about it?'"

At this point, DeFelice says, the student is starting to feel some compassion for the teacher. "Now we can try to get to the real root of the problem," he concludes. "What made the child angry? Is it a problem at

Teachers have
a boiling point.

home? Is the child insecure? I can't *make* them tell me. They have to want to tell me, and I've got to make them know they're loved first."

Modeling this approach, according to DeFelice, he used to see from six to 10 students a day for discipline issues. Over the next year, it went down to one or two a week. "It got to the point where kids would break down and cry because they had disappointed me or a teacher. They weren't upset that they'd been caught. They were sad because they knew they could do better."

With this kind of growth, DeFelice continues, sometimes students would even coach each other: "I have a parrot in my office and kids often come in for a visit. Occasionally another student would be sent in for a discipline problem. I'd say to the first kid, 'Why don't you talk to this little man and tell him how we do things here?'

"Ultimately, more and more kids came to my office not for discipline but to tell me about the book they read or show off one of their papers. Man, I love those office visits."

A cool place to be

In other cases, DeFelice admits, discipline issues may also be related to a lack of Play. "If we're just cranking worksheets all day long, nobody's having any fun, including the teachers. If I'm learning multiplication tables, I'd rather do it in a game or in a hands-on way."

The problem comes, he explains, when kids get a little wound up or the teacher gets frustrated. "The teacher says, 'Oh you're gonna run around, huh? Well, I'll fix you: Here's another worksheet!' And it becomes gruesome, drudgery, laborious—and the worse it gets, so does the kids' behavior," DeFelice says. "So we've got to continually look at our objective: What am I trying to accomplish here? If kids learn more when they're having fun, maybe we have to take some risks and loosen the reins a little."

This kind of colorful, playful environment can make all the

difference for some children. "Let me tell you about this kid," DeFelice says. "I just fell in love with him. The first day he came to register, I jumped on the floor, got on my knees and said, 'Hey, how you doin'? I'm Mr. D, your principal. I want to be your new best friend!' He just beamed. He was bouncing with energy. I'm kind of hyperactive, too, so we hit it off.

"I'd see him running down the hall and he'd practically jump into my arms and say, 'I'm going to get another book from the library!' I'd say, 'You are the coolest kid I ever met!' Oh, he was antsy and talkative sometimes, but it was nothing his teacher couldn't deal with.

"Then one day I met a teacher from his *previous* school. I said, 'Hey, you sent us a great kid! I love that kid!' She said, 'You're kidding. He was the *worst* student in our school.'

"'In what way?!' I said. 'In *every* way,' she chided. 'Troublemaker. Talking. Bad attitude.'

"Later I saw the student and I said, 'Hey buddy, you're one of the coolest human beings I know. But I understand you had some problems at your old school. If you don't mind me askin', what's the difference?'

"And he said, 'Look around, Mr. D! Everything we do here is cool. We've got the goldfish pond. We've got gardens and plants everywhere. We do fun stuff. This is a cool place to be.'

"Many of these kids put up with a lot, but they are so resilient. They don't hold grudges. All you have to do is show them you care and create an environment that gives them hope."

> "I'm kind of hyperactive, too, so we hit it off."

Showing respect, making friends

This caring, committed approach extends to Boundary Street's interactions with parents too. "Parents need hope, like everybody else," DeFelice explains. "When they come in, the first thing I do is tell them about all the good things their child is doing. I tell them that the fact that they're at school shows how much they care about their children."

If the meeting is about a discipline problem, DeFelice makes sure to get out of his chair and greet parents and students in front of his desk. "I'd get down on my hands and knees, and kneel, talking to the child at eye level. Now we'd be on an equal playing field. Instead of lording it over them, I'm almost subservient.

"See, you've got to understand that many parents in high-poverty schools either didn't finish school or didn't have a good experience with school. When they come in they're either intimidated or don't like you; in their experience, school is the bad guy. For these parents to see you on your knees talking to their child in a loving and gentle way, it makes all the difference in the world."

After time, he continues, "It got to the point where parents would come in angry, and we're hugging when they walk out. Or I'd give the dads a good pat on the back and a handshake. I've affirmed them and their child, and we've worked to find the best solution for everyone. I've chosen my attitude, tried to be there for them, and it's made their day.

"Now I don't want you thinkin' it's always a bed of roses around here," he adds. "I thought one guy was going to hit me in the face, he was so mad. I didn't want him to break my new glasses so I took them off and put them behind my back.

"Plus," DeFelice laughs, "I'm blind as a bat so if I don't see the punch coming, it's not gonna hurt as bad."

"I thought one guy was going to hit me in the face ..."

Keeping hope alive

The staff's positive focus at Boundary Street Elementary has made a major difference, in and outside school. In May 2004, it was one of just 78 South Carolina schools to receive the Red Carpet award from the State Department of Education for its family-friendly, service-focused, and welcoming atmosphere. The department also recognized Boundary Street with a Palmetto Gold award for academic improvement, an award given to just 229 out of 1,100 schools.

So all of the school's problems have been solved, right? Not quite, DeFelice says. The school's challenges haven't changed. "There's still poverty, drugs at home, struggling single parents, some of them not much older than high school kids. The school still has a high transient rate," he says.

In addition, a large number of children still come to school performing below grade level; some of them are even several months behind. "The staff does a great job helping our kids catch up," DeFelice says. "By the time they leave their grade, many of them will have made more than a year's worth of progress—like a year and three month's worth—but they're still not at grade level. So our state report card says our academic performance is still deficient. What's even crazier is because of some weird arbitrary standards, we didn't even get to include our highest-performing students."

All of this takes a psychological toll. "These are the children with whom our teachers want to work and the community with whom they want to work," he says. "But it's easy to feel the external pressure and negative stereotype that you're not doing a good job because you're not getting the best report card grade.

"When you've been at the bottom for decades," DeFelice adds, "it can creep into your head that, 'Hey, maybe we *can't* do any better.' We've got to constantly guard against that thinking. Because we *can* do better."

According to DeFelice, The FISH! Philosophy has reminded the staff to keep speaking this language of hope. "It's not all FISH!, but the philosophy is closely intertwined with our educational and discipline strategies. It's helped us make a major mind-shift that always keeps us pointed to the positive. Look, we're not knights in shining armor, but I think we are a glimmer of hope. Just knowing that keeps us going."

A teacher who is
attempting to teach
without inspiring
the pupil with a desire
to learn is hammering
on a cold iron.

—*Horace Mann*

 **THOUGHT**

WHO ARE *YOU* BEING?

Educators have enough on their plates already, but The FISH! Philosophy isn't about doing anything extra. It's about who you are being while you're doing what you're doing.

Doing is necessary, but it's easy to get wrapped up in all of our doings. When that happens we may feel rushed and impatient. "Being" in The FISH! Philosophy means thinking about and taking responsibility for how you react to the world around you, how you treat others, how you treat yourself.

When we focus on being who we want to be, it changes how we see the world around us. We are free to deal with challenging students and situations more calmly— and the right path seems to show up. Choosing who you are going to be is the most important commitment there is.

"I Caught the Baby on the Way Out"

The students in Denise Mileson's class worry about different things than most teenagers.

"Sometimes the tears come because the boy who fathered their child, the one who was going to be there forever, has a new girlfriend and won't be involved anymore," Denise says. "Sometimes it's arguments with parents who are still furious about the pregnancy. For some girls, it's 'How am I going to make it on my own because my parents kicked me out?' The other day, a student was thinking about placing her four-month-old up for adoption because she's struggling in so many ways."

Denise works with young parents at the Tri-Tech Skills Center in Kennewick, Washington. The center, which serves seven area school districts, offers high school and college credit in such classes as pre-nursing, graphic design, law enforcement, and auto tech.

Denise's students range in age from 14 to 21. Most are female. Some are pregnant and working to graduate. Some dropped out to have a baby and decided to return. Most are at the center half-days and attend their home high schools the rest of the day. Many also hold down jobs.

"They know they didn't make the best choice," Denise says. "In fact, especially after they've had the baby, they know that choice has made their lives really difficult.

"Before, most of them didn't see a need for education. They were kids, it was their chance in life to party. But once these kids get pregnant, their focus changes. A lot of them tell me, 'I wish my life could have changed, without me getting pregnant, because I was on a road to destruction. But once I became pregnant, it forced me to look at my priorities because now I had to get my act together.'"

That's the focus of Denise's class: "'Where are you going? How are you going to get there?' That pops up in almost everything we do," she says.

A new way of thinking

Besides math and English skills, Denise's students study the fundamentals of a healthy pregnancy, infant growth and development, and how to care for a newborn. They learn how to get a job, write a resume, and find childcare. They discuss discipline, abuse, and the importance of feeling good about yourself, whether a parent or a child.

They also learn The FISH! Philosophy. "At first the kids didn't know what to make of it," Denise says. "For some of them being cool is still pretty important, so images of throwing fish and acting silly was a hard concept. It took a while and it took some thought. But they started to embrace it." The first principle that showed up, Denise says, was Be There.

Students often think no one else has ever gone through the problem they're facing, but usually one or two classmates have been through similar situations and can offer support. "Sometimes we offer advice," she says, "and sometimes there's nothing we can do but listen and let them know we're there."

One day, a student needed to take her baby to a doctor in Seattle. The student's mother was supposed to take her, but backed out at the last minute. Another student volunteered to drive her. The next day the two young mothers, with their infants, made the five-hour trip together.

Later, in class, Denise's students talked about why the driver would do that, especially since they weren't the best of friends. "There's not a lot of stuff I can do for people," the volunteer explained, "but I had a car, she had money for gas, and we stayed with one of her relatives. We could get along if we had to. She needed somebody—and it turned out to be me."

To teach the power of Make Their Day, Denise introduced a weekly activity where students draw the name of a classmate and secretly buy them something. The gift can't cost more than a dollar.

"The kids think it's pretty cool," Denise says. "One girl was so excited. She told me, 'I just love trying to figure out what's gonna Make Their Day. It's worth it for that feeling.' Her mom and aunt are in prison and her boyfriend's in jail. Her life is hard. And *she's* excited about making somebody else's day."

Choose Your Attitude also especially resonates with many of Denise's students. "Some kids have so much going against them outside of school that they have to consciously let it go when they arrive each day," she says. "Choice is all they have."

This doesn't make the choosing any easier. One student was taking her problems out on anyone within earshot when Denise reminded her that she could choose her attitude. "Whatever!" she yelled and stormed out of class. An hour later the student returned. "That was the last thing I wanted to hear you say," she admitted.

"I know," Denise said quietly.

"Well, I needed to hear you say it … but it was the last thing I wanted to hear."

"Her mom and aunt are in prison … and *she's* excited about making somebody else's day."

Build the relationship first

According to Denise, some teachers are afraid to substitute in her class. "It's because I have *those kids*," she says. "I think they're awesome but you have to take the time to establish trust. It's about the relationship first. Establish the relationship and teaching the class is easy.

"We start every class talking about respect. I listen when they talk to me. I don't judge them. I'm honest and they know I won't ever lie to them. At the end of every day I take inventory: 'Did I make some contact with each student today?'"

While Denise says she has few discipline problems, there are occasional "chats." "I tell them, 'If I ask you to stop by my office, it could mean you have a phone call, it could mean I want to tell you how lovely you are, or it might mean we need to have a chat.'"

After a few weeks the kids feel safe to be completely honest. "We were talking about discipline," Denise says. "I posed the question, 'What do you do if your child gets into your makeup and spills it all over the floor?'"

"I'd slap him!" a 14-year-old student blurted out.

"She was totally serious and the class kind of got on her," Denise says. "Later on, while the kids were working on their assignments, I sat with her and said there are better ways to discipline than slapping."

"But getting slapped was all I ever knew growing up," the girl said. "This is all new to me."

Laughing through the tears

With stories like this, Denise admits she has hard days. "I have to make a conscious choice that everything's going to be fine, and I tell the kids that," she says. "Some days I have to laugh about things others would cry about."

Like the call she got from a student who had just graduated. "She has a 16-month-old and she told me she was pregnant again. All I could say was, 'You're kidding!' I want to whack her, but I can't, so I'll support her. She knows I don't like that she's pregnant again, but she knows I won't abandon her either."

There are distinct rewards too. "I get to teach them about raising and loving children," Denise says. "They call me when they have their babies. A couple of times I was there when students delivered and that was amazing. One student called from the hospital and said, 'Can you come over? I don't think I can make it.' I was with her through the night. The other one, I actually *caught* the baby on the way out! The doctor was still washing up!"

Over the years, Denise has learned that being a teacher involves much more than preparing lesson plans ... like having to tell a student, in the midst of a custody battle for her baby, that a family member with a court order had taken the child from school. "It's the hardest thing I've ever done in my life," Denise recalls. "When she found out, she collapsed on the floor and started screaming, 'No! No!'—like someone had died. I just held her."

"It was an amazing thing for a 17-year-old to have to go through."

Denise arranged counseling for the student, after which the girl gathered affidavits that supported her case in court. Less than two weeks later, the student had her baby back. "She got a lawyer but had already done most of the work on her own," Denise says. "It was an amazing thing for a 17-year-old to have to go through."

Later the girl told Denise, "You are my mother."

"I can't be your mother," Denise said gently. "I am your teacher and, after you graduate, I will always be your friend."

The power of belief

According to Denise, the most important thing she can give her students is the knowledge that she believes in them so they will learn to believe in themselves. "Two years ago, I had a student who had been into drugs and was just starting to clean up her act," she says. "She was very negative about life, only came to school enough to stay enrolled, and would go off on people at the drop of a dime.

"When she had her baby, she started to focus. And she had people who believed in her. Her foster parents believed in her. I believed in her. Another teacher at the center believed in her.

"When she left me to go back to her home high school, she told me, in no uncertain terms, 'I *will* graduate.' Sure enough, I was at the senior graduation party and saw her. 'It took me six years,' the student said, 'but here I am.' To which I said, 'Never had a doubt.'

"She would tell you she didn't have a choice about graduating, that we didn't give her a choice. But *she's* the one who made the choice."

The FISH! Philosophy has helped Denise's students recognize this choice—and their own power. "It's made class more fun. Now we can speak the same language and all the kids understand it. Now, when we type job resumes, under Special Skills, some will put 'The FISH! Philosophy.'"

Denise shares another example. "We did an assignment to compare how you were raised with how you plan to raise your child, and students wrote things like, 'I'm going to Be There and listen to my child when they talk to me. I'm going to choose my attitude every morning before I start dealing with my baby.' Wow. How powerful would it be if *all* parents did that?"

With stories like these, Denise remains fully committed to her students' growth—and gifts—everyday. "With these kids you get back so much more than they take. And people say to me, 'How can you keep working with these kids?'" she says. "I tell them, 'I don't know how I *cannot* keep working with them.'"

"I *will* graduate!"

Everywhere, we learn only from those whom we love.

—Johann Wolfgang von Goethe

 **THOUGHT**

NEW DAY, NEW CHOICES

Too often we judge others, especially students, on their past choices, as if those choices predict the future. But their choices are based on what they have been taught, not on what they have yet to learn.

John Gardner, quoted in the book *FISH!*, offers words that every educator might pass on to students: "There is something about you that you may not even know about yourself. You have within you more resources of energy than have ever been tapped, more talent than has ever been exploited, more strength than has ever been tested, and more to give than you have ever been given."

The beauty of Choose Your Attitude is that if yesterday was full of bad decisions, you get to make new ones today. The challenge is that if you made good choices yesterday, you must do it all over again. See your students as the choices they have the potential to make and they are more likely to live into your expectations.

"Give a Little Part of Yourself"

Every student is different, but they all want the same thing.

"Kids today are just like we were," says Steve Colorio of Seven Hills Charter School in Worcester, Massachusetts. "You know when you were in school, the teachers that mattered most were the ones who'd pull you aside and ask about the little things: 'How'd your game go?' Or 'Nice shirt. Where'd you get it?' Or 'Did you watch the Red Sox game last night?' It's just this and that—but it makes all the difference.

"When you're there for kids, the little ones gather around you like you're a Disney character at a theme park. All you have to say is 'How you doin'?' and they're like 'Mr. C! Mr. C!' and they want to shake your hand. If they were feeling down, they smile and you've just changed their mood for the day. And you have the power to do that, to plant positive seeds."

Steve is the behavior management specialist for Seven Hills, which serves a diverse population in grades kindergarten through eighth. "I may not be the smartest guy around," he says. "But I do know that if you know how to relate to kids, they will buy what you're selling, and you can make a difference.

"That why I like The FISH! Philosophy," he continues. "It's part of my repertoire. It's what I can bring to the table because FISH! is what's in your soul and your heart. Kids are a quick study. They see what's going on inside you. If you're full of fun and passion and compassion, and you're honest and fair and caring, they're with you. You'll get the job done."

Making others better

Steve's favorite principle is Choose Your Attitude. "As long as you make the kids your number one priority, don't worry about the staff, the administration, the parents. Choose the attitude that you're going to do the right thing for the right reason and everything falls into place the right way. It may not always seem like it at the time but if you really trust that, it seems to work out."

And good choices usually get passed on. "We had a kid in school who was kind of socially awkward," Steve recalls. "He had to go in front of the class and do a presentation about a story he'd written and he was really nervous. I saw this coming, so I pulled one of the cool guys aside.

"I said to this kid, 'Listen, I know you don't know him but he's gonna give this speech, and maybe you could ask him some questions about it.' He said, 'I don't have any questions to ask him, Mr. C.' I said, 'Think about if you were up there and how hard it is. You have all these friends. It's easy for you, but it may not be easy for him. All I'm asking is that you think about it.'

"He said, 'I don't know.' I told him, 'It's up to you. Nobody's gonna fault you for it.'

"So class begins. The students start giving their speeches. Finally this socially awkward kid gets up and starts doing his thing. He's really nervous but he gets through it and he goes, 'Are there any questions?' It was so quiet it was like you could hear crickets in the middle of the night. Every other student had gotten questions. I'm in the back, thinking, 'Oh, man.'

"Suddenly this cool kid raises his hand. 'Ummm ... did you like doing this story?' he says. The kid in front says, 'Yeah, I loved doing it. My mom helped me with it.' All of a sudden another student raises his hand. 'What made you want to write about this?' Before you knew it, another kid raised his hand and then another. There weren't a ton of questions but enough to make it a very positive experience for this student.

"It was important that this other kid's question paved the way for that," Steve interjects. "Because I've seen this before, where one bad experience in class creates a situation where you don't want to go in front of an audience anymore and it goes into adulthood and life is a little harder.

"After class was over, I pulled the cool kid aside and said, 'Sleep well tonight. You made all the difference in the world with that kid. It's one thing to make great choices and it's another to make great choices that make others better. You made someone better today.'

"He said, 'All I did was ask a question.' I said, 'That's all you had to do.'

"The greatest thing you can give another person isn't money or anything like that," Steve says. "The best thing you can give is a little something of yourself."

"The best thing you can give is a little something of yourself."

Do you ever do something to make someone else's day?

Yeah, I ask them if they want to play.

Why do you do that?

To make them happy.

How do you feel when you've made them happy?

Proud of myself.

—*Kenny, a second grader*

The Attitude Board

It was a special day at Antheil Elementary School. The New Jersey deputy commissioner of education was visiting and about to read a story to Bob Kohut's third grade class.

Suddenly one of the students raised his hand and asked, "Did you put your fish up on the board yet?"

The deputy commissioner looked perplexed, until the third grader explained. "We have an attitude board. Whenever we come in our room, we choose a fish. They're different colors 'cause each one stands for a different feeling. There's happy, confident, sad, or angry. We put our fish up so we are aware of the attitudes we're choosing here."

The deputy commissioner smiled with new understanding. "Actually, I'm quite happy today," he said, and he put the happy fish up.

"That was awesome, because the attitude board is part of what we do every day and the student wanted to share it," Bob says. "When the deputy commissioner read to the kids, they were totally there for him. No one had to be reminded to pay attention, and he really noticed."

A license to be me

It wasn't always like this, however. As principal Joan Zuckerman notes, when she came to Antheil Elementary several years ago, she saw the increasingly challenging needs of its students—and a staff working to keep up.

"Many of our students come from stable homes, but others leave school each day not always knowing where they're going to sleep that night. Simply punishing Susie with no recess for not getting her homework done, when there was no one home to help her get her homework done, wasn't going to work anymore," she explains.

Bob comments from a teacher's perspective: "I know there were days if I went in and wasn't feeling great, if the first thing I did was jump on somebody, that set the tone for the day," he says. "The kids weren't necessarily with me through the lesson and I didn't give my best lessons either, because I was beating myself up for jumping on a kid or still stuck in whatever I was unhappy about."

One day a colleague dropped by Joan's office and popped a *FISH!* video into her VCR. "I didn't want to watch it because I had just gotten back from vacation and had e-mails and voice mails to answer. I was arguing with her about it but by then they were throwing fish. And my comment was probably the same as everyone else's: 'What are we going to throw?'" Joan says. "I wasn't sure it would work here. Then someone asked, 'What makes you think your workplace is any different from anybody else's?'"

Joan introduced The FISH! Philosophy to her staff in September 2001. Reactions were mixed. One teacher said, "This is a language that fits who I want to be!" Another teacher wondered if she could roller-skate in the halls now. Bob instantly connected with it.

"On my father's side," he explains, "basically everyone was in the Teamsters. On my mother's side were laborers who did exhausting,

> "This is a language that fits who I want to be!"

repetitious jobs. To see these fish guys *deciding* to be happy, I knew I could do that in my classroom. I felt this was a license to be me, turned up a notch. This isn't trying to change me. It's just me without filters."

Creating FISH! lessons

Within a few days Bob showed *FISH!* to his third graders. "They got it immediately. We talked about how we could bring it into our lives at school."

One of the class's first FISH! ideas was the attitude board. "It's been a great way to remind each other that we are responsible for our choices," Bob says. "Even if you've chosen that attitude right now, you can change it if it isn't working. When you are clear about the fact that you are making a choice, you tend not to stay in that negative frame of mind as long."

Bob talked with his class about how, if students put up angry or sad, it's their choice—and they have a right to it. "The kids tell me if someone puts up angry, they try to give that student a little more space. So it cut down on confrontation. If they noticed a classmate put up a sad fish—and it stayed up for a while—they'd see if they could do anything to help.

"If I see that a student is putting up sad or angry a few days in a row, I'll ask if they want to talk about it. One time I noticed a kid was putting up angry on Mondays a lot. I asked him about it. His parents aren't together and he was angry that on weekends he gets to see mom but then when Monday comes he's not going to see her for a few days. Just being able to talk about it helped him understand his feelings and deal with them."

Bob especially gets a kick out of checking the board on test days. "If it's filled with confident and happy fish, it's an accurate indicator that students will do well."

"She held the door open"

Bob's students also keep daily journals, reflecting on what they've done to make someone else's day and what someone else has done to make theirs. Often students decided to share their entries.

"One day one of the quietest girls in my class was struggling because she said she hadn't done anything to make anyone's day. I had the rest of the class stop writing, mentioned her dilemma, and asked if anyone could share how she had made their day. Six or seven hands shot up and her classmates said things like: 'She held the door open for me when my arms were full of books.' 'She laughed at my joke.' 'She stood in line for me because I had crutches.'

"A huge smile spread across her face. Not only had she made their day, but they had made hers."

Play happens

Play is the FISH! principle the class talks about least. "For us, it just happens," Bob says. "It happens when we're doing the other things—choosing our attitudes, being there, making people's day. If we do that, kids are feeling good and Play comes naturally." Like the day a spelling lesson turned into an impromptu sing-along.

"Someone was spelling a word, and one of the kids said all I can think of is the song 'B-I-N-G-O'. So the kids started spelling words to the tune of 'B-I-N-G-O'. Other times they sing the spelling of the word, and then we guess the tune they've sung the word to."

"B-I-N-G-O!"

Bob explains another learning game the kids invented. "We have a large map of the U.S. on our playground. When we were studying the 50 states, a student asked if I would quiz him on the states using the large map, which is unlabeled. Before I knew it, several other kids asked me to quiz them—and this was at recess! Our vice principal saw the kids playing a game on the map where someone calls out the name of a state, and the first kid to get on that state stays on."

He adds, "We're very serious about learning; Play is just how we feel while we're doing it."

From relationship to responsibility

Bob has learned that social skills aren't separate from academic success; they are the path to it. "I have never yet had a student leave my third grade classroom and go directly to college or the job market. They've got a lot of time left to learn the academics. In the meantime they need life skills — how to work with others, becoming confident in themselves. If they don't have those skills, it's much harder to learn the academics later."

Bob weaves these lessons into his curriculum. "Sometimes we'll read a story and I'll ask, 'How might the story have changed if this character had chosen a different attitude? How did this character's actions make the other character's day?' Their reading comprehension is better and they're doing higher-level thinking."

These theoretic discussions impact real-life behavior. "It's not uncommon for students to ask me, 'Can I talk to this person because we're having some problems?' I'll say, 'Sure, if you need me, you know where I am.' Now they solve a lot of their problems without me. In the past I'd want to take control of situations like that, get it resolved: *'You sit over here! You sit over here! Done.'* But in the meantime, you've missed an opportunity for them to learn about relationships and how to deal with other people."

In the process many students develop a strong sense of ownership for their classroom. "When I'd arrive in the morning I noticed that our lockers were open and ready for the students, chairs had been taken down from the desks, and the classroom was basically ready to go.

"One day, when I came in, I found this kid putting down chairs. He

"They solve a lot of their problems without me."

comes in for the early breakfast program. He's been in some trouble before. I asked, 'Have you been doing this for a while?' He said, 'Yes,' and I said, 'Thank you. I really appreciate it. You saved me a lot of time.'

"So we got into a routine. I'd go up front to sign in and make some copies and he'd get the room ready. If we had papers to pass out, I'd leave them with him and he'd put one on every desk. I learned I have to take some chances with these kids. There's no other way for them to learn responsibility."

Choosing to help

This level of responsibility—for themselves and others—sets a tone for Bob's class as they recite their daily pledge:

I will have a good day today. I feel good about who I am today. I feel good about who you are today.

I will do my best to understand, accept, and appreciate myself and others.

I will choose my attitude, be there for others, and try to make someone's day today.

And no one, and no one, and NO ONE, can change that.

These words never rang truer than when Bob's students began working with one of Antheil's classes for children with autism.

Before they started, Bob explains, "The teacher of that class read my kids a story about autism and answered their questions. We said if you choose not to play with them, that's your choice. But we don't want you to feel sorry for them and try to do everything for them. If you feel like it, just be their friend.

"My kids taught one of the children with autism how to swing—something her teachers hadn't been able to do. If we're in science, my students will just put a hand on their shoulder and talk to them quietly. Sometimes they take their hands to teach them how to high-five other kids.

"Because of what our kids have learned through The FISH!

"My kids taught one of the children with autism how to swing."

Philosophy, I've never seen them lose their patience or get upset. Children with autism sometimes have a hard time knowing what's appropriate or expressing themselves. You've got to be fully present to connect with them—and these kids have been there 100 percent."

Spreading the joy

The FISH! Philosophy has also helped the staff Be There for one another. Bob explains, "Two weeks after we were introduced to FISH!, 9-11 happened. We had students whose families were affected, teachers who were in a panic because they couldn't get in touch with relatives who either worked in the World Trade Center or nearby.

"Of course we would have been there for each other without knowing about FISH!, but knowing the language made it easier down the road to talk about it and understand how important it is."

The Antheil staff has faced many Be There tests since then. The next year, the day before school started, one of the most respected teachers in the building suffered a stroke. Over just a few months, five staff members lost loved ones. One lost her daughter *and* her husband. The vice principal lost her husband suddenly; she was pregnant with their first child.

When their colleagues were struggling, the Antheil staff covered their classes, helped substitutes, organized lesson plans, completed paperwork, and updated students. They prepared meals to bring to the families. "We started to feel more like a family, even people who hadn't been particularly friendly with each other," Joan says.

"Today," Bob adds, "I see more people offering to help each other. Teachers from different grade levels do lessons together. Instead of just passing each other in the hallways, I see more people being there for each other in conversations."

With FISH!, the staff has also gotten permission to loosen up, though Bob says it took time. "At first some people didn't always feel safe

"We started to feel more like a family…"

playing because they were embarrassed. Or they had this ultra-serious persona so long that they thought if I do Play, it's going to seem like I'm not professional anymore."

Joan worried about the same thing. "When I first presented FISH!, instead of saying we can have fun, I kept saying *respectful* fun, as though the two didn't go together. My fear was that the fun might get out of hand. But it hasn't. Not even close. I finally realized that of course our staff is going to be respectful and responsible. We know we have an important job to do, and we do it better by making it fun."

Visitors have noticed this energy. "A parent whose child transferred here said that at the child's previous school, she just always felt like things were about to erupt," Joan says. "She said here when you meet people in the hall, whether it's teachers or kids, they actually *talk* to you."

Joan never mandated The FISH! Philosophy. "I just tried to let everyone who had ideas go with them," she says. That's why FISH! has never seemed like a program.

"It's more of a mindset," Bob adds. "It's something that's working for us, and it's appreciated and valued."

"Inside it,
Bob's students had
drawn pictures
and written special
messages."

Mr. Kohut is always there

Bob's students and parents showed how much they valued his efforts when their nomination led to his selection as Antheil's Teacher of the Year. With the help of his colleagues, they created a special book and unveiled it at a surprise party. Inside it, Bob's students had drawn pictures and written special messages.

One read: *Mr. Kohut is funny. I think he likes teaching.* Said another: *He shows us how to solve our own problems, but if we need him, he's always there.*

One of his students wrote: *I'll miss you when I go to fourth grade. Is there any way you can advance to fourth grade?*

The secret in education lies in respecting the student.

—Ralph Waldo Emerson

 **THOUGHT**

THE *REAL* SELF-ESTEEM

The notion of self-esteem has taken a battering in recent years. To many, it means heaping children with undeserved praise or assigning tasks so unchallenging that they will always succeed. The goal, it seems, is to make sure no one ever feels bad.

But this usually leads to an inflated sense of ones's abilities—and that's not self-esteem. For example, in a study of how students around the world felt about their math competency, Americans scored highest in self-image but lowest in actual proficiency. Confidence that is not backed up by skill keeps students from reaching their potential as much as having skill but not the confidence to use it. Children who never have to deal with failure or never learn from mistakes don't get the chance to develop the self-reliance and sense of accomplishment that comes from actually overcoming obstacles.

Noted author and psychotherapist Nathaniel Branden has defined self-esteem as knowing you are "competent to cope with the basic challenges of life" and "worthy of happiness." Such inner strength makes it possible to handle criticism, make healthy choices, and be accountable for how you treat yourself and others (Choose Your Attitude); to try new things and take risks (Play); and to know you are loved and, in that self-confidence, to love and respect others (Be There and Make Their Day).

Students deserve to be pushed, to accomplish more than they thought possible. They may succeed on the first try, but mostly they'll need support to pick themselves up and try again. As educators, we can't simply award self-esteem to students, but we can create conditions in which they are given the chance to earn it for themselves.

A TEACHER'S PURPOSE

A Place Kids
Don't Want to Leave

At David St. Germain's first teaching interview at a school in northern Minnesota, the principal asked him, "What word best describes what learning should be?"

"Fun," David earnestly replied.

The principal shook his head wearily. "Son, you will never get a teaching job with that answer," he said. "Education is not fun. It's damned hard work and don't you forget it."

David didn't get that job, but he took the message to heart as a young English teacher at Chaska High School in the early 1970s. "Everyone told me you've got to be meaner than a junkyard dog the first day. 'Sit down, here are my rules, turn to page six—boom, boom, boom.' It wasn't who I wanted to be, but it was the way I was taught."

Fast forward

A few years later, David had been hired as a teacher and debate coach, but he was still trying to get into his groove as an educator. One night, as he drove home from debate practice, he wondered, "I love coaching debate but I don't like teaching in the classroom. Why?"

Determined, he started analyzing the evolution of his coaching style. "In coaching debate," he reasoned, "I used to give them what I thought was the winning argument. And they'd go into the room and I wouldn't hear them use that argument. I'd ask, 'What happened to the economic growth argument?' They'd say they forgot … or they hadn't really understood it.

"I learned it didn't work to just give orders. I had to collaborate with them to understand why one strategy was better than another. After each competition, we'd talk about it: 'How did that work for you?' 'What might you try next time in that situation?'"

This approach created a relationship. "I was still the coach and they were still my debaters, but we worked as partners. I chose an attitude of collaboration and fun. I wanted them to want to come back to debate every night. The more I partnered with them, the harder they worked. They came after school, researched their debate topics on their own—which was exactly what I wanted to see more of in the classroom."

In time, David decided to bring this same approach to his classroom. "I had been trained and the students had been trained that I needed to be in control. Well, you can always get obedience. All you need is a bigger stick. But it only works if you're in the room. I wanted a classroom where kids felt safe, where we had fun, where they wanted to take personal responsibility for their actions and their learning. And I started to do some things differently.

"The catch was," David notes, "that we needed to get through content. I had as much time with the debate team as we all wanted. I only had 55 minutes each day with my students in class. I couldn't just say to the next teacher, 'I'm sorry we didn't get to prepositional phrases, you'll have to pick that up for me.' I needed a way to get across the things I was doing with my debate team in a shorter amount of time."

"I only had
55 minutes each day
with my students."

A new language

In 1998, David saw the *FISH!* video for the first time. "Within the first few minutes, I knew this was what I needed. Here was a video that in less than 20 minutes covered everything I wanted. We'd been talking about fun and that was Play. We wanted to be more positive and that was Choose Your Attitude. We needed more recognition and that was Make Their Day. Be There was how we communicated with each other. It was a pretty easy fit. I showed it to my wife, Sally, who was trying to accomplish the same things with elementary kids in the district, and she agreed: This is something that will work with kids of all ages. We both dove in."

As the *FISH!* video is too often shown once, discussed briefly, then never seen again, David knew the philosophy is not an automatic fix. "We knew from Bloom's taxonomy that you have to do a behavior 30 times before it becomes a habit. People don't change; they gradually become accustomed to doing things a different way."

To begin, adopting FISH! required a paradigm shift. "Actually putting this philosophy into practice can be threatening. You have to want to care about others. If you think teaching is about things and data, it may frighten you. My paradigm shift came when I recognized that if these kids were not in the room, I wouldn't have a job. They're my customers and I'm serving them. Some teachers, frankly, see it the other way."

David decided to weave The FISH! Philosophy into his day-to-day approach, developing discussions and activities that let students consider these behaviors, try them on, and decide if they want to keep them. Sally did the same with her elementary students in the Chaska district.

> "My paradigm shift came when I recognized that if these kids were not in the room, I wouldn't have a job."

Play = safety

For David, the first step in building a partnering relationship with his students was through a social contract. "Most conflicts are about differing expectations," he says. "The students and I need to get clear on those up front. It doesn't take much time, maybe an hour, but it sets a tone that this is important."

Handing out rules, however, is *not* a way to define mutual expectations. "This is a conversation about what works for *everyone* in the classroom, and *everyone* must agree," David says. "I'm not here to be a guard. I'm not here to be a higher moral power. I'm a member of this community, just as each student is. I may have more professional and life experience, but I'm a learner in here too. If we don't have that conversation, I'm just teaching them as opposed to them becoming active learners."

In that conversation, The FISH! Philosophy becomes a goal to shoot for every day. "It's hard to be nasty and say you're being there. Or to say that you're choosing your attitude, yet you're always grumpy. FISH! becomes a mirror of how we are treating each other. Usually we see, as we talk, that we share many responsibilities. Our roles may be different, but our responsibilities in creating a welcoming culture, in being there for each other, are basically the same."

As the social contract defines expectations for how the people in the class will treat one another, the classroom becomes a safer place for everyone—adults included. "I remember spelling a word wrong on the board—it was *ambiguous*—and the class laughed at me," David says. "I was devastated. I thought, 'What if this gets out?' Finally, I thought, 'If I'm so uptight that I can't make a mistake or trip in the classroom or tell a joke, I'm not being real.'

"Now, the other part of this is that the kids laughed at me. I had to talk with them, because that didn't work for me. So we had a conversation about it and they understood how I felt. When I wasn't sure how to spell a word, I'd say, 'Can you help me out here?' They were a little shocked, but it created a new relationship. Suddenly I could be myself."

Kids need to be able to be themselves in class too. David recalls, "In high school, because of alphabetical seating, I repeatedly sat next to the same girl, who was a perfect student. When she diagrammed sentences or did math problems, it was art. When I was called to the board, just after her, it looked like chicken scratching. I didn't ever feel confident in those classes.

"A lot of students feel the same way. They're afraid to answer a question wrong. Maybe they don't feel safe because of something that happened in third grade with another kid in class. Or the teacher puts them down or embarrasses them. You can't learn when you're afraid; you just shut down.

"That's why, to me, Play is the most misunderstood FISH! concept. A lot of people think Play is just about fun and being silly. I think it's about feeling safe to take a chance with learning, to know you're accepted no matter what. In our class, we can do that because through our social contract, we've agreed on standards. That keeps Play in line. If we're not being there, making their day, and choosing our attitude when we Play, it doesn't work."

According to David, FISH! highlights the core of safety—trust. "If we don't have trust, we don't have anything. When we trust each other, we can approach things with a lighthearted attitude, welcome other people's ideas, and be ourselves."

"Teachers outside of school laugh and have fun, and in class they're so serious it hurts."

And being yourself is key to effective teaching. "One of my students said she sees teachers outside school laughing and having fun, and in class they are so serious it hurts. I know teachers who put on a different persona at school than they do in the rest of their lives. That's what I was doing. If you're not being real, you can't teach—because you're living a lie. It's exhausting.

"So if you like to tell jokes, go with that. If not, don't force it. The kids can see through it and so can you. It's uncomfortable—and you've got to be comfortable in the classroom."

Be There = asking

In the early 1980s, in addition to his teaching assignment, David became the professional development coordinator at Chaska High School. "In that role I got a lot of questions about discipline," he says. "The main one was: 'How can I fix this kid who's driving me crazy?'"

David read everything he could on discipline. He observed his fellow teachers. He observed himself. And one thing became clear: "Teachers have been conditioned to control. When students act up or don't do what you want, you nail 'em. Likewise, kids are trained in the paradigm that if you don't obey, you get punished—with yelling, a low grade, or detention.

"I'd read kids the riot act. It seemed like a quick fix and I felt like I did something. It was so tempting: 'You wanna argue with *me*? Go ahead! I'm the *debate* coach!' But it's like crack ... You get a temporary high but pretty quickly you don't feel so good—and if you do, you're in the wrong profession!

"Some kids get *their* needs met by arguing with you," he continues. "They won't admit to anything—and why would they if their only option is getting punished? So you spend your time arguing, and pretty soon you're focused more on the argument than you are the original behavior. Even if you win, you lose. Kids will obey you—until you leave the room. Plus you lose any chance of developing the kind of relationship that might help you reach their hearts."

For David, the answer was to spend less time telling students what to do, and more time asking what *they* thought they should do. "It's simple questions like, 'What happened?' 'What did you want to have happen?' 'How's that working for you?'"

Teachers would never think of depriving students of the chance to learn academic lessons. But when they yell or tell, they basically deprive students of the chance to learn responsibility. "Some kids would rather have detention than have to answer questions, because they don't have to *think* in detention," David says.

Choosing the appropriate attitude is important when asking

"But it's like crack ..."

questions, he adds. "If I get angry, I may ask a question but it comes out like, 'What the hell are you doing!!!?' That's a very different question than if I calmly ask, 'What are you doing?' It's a major paradigm shift."

David, however, doesn't advise asking questions when breaking up a fight. "If someone's safety is at risk, of course you act first and talk later. But 95 percent of problems in school are not dangerous—it's kids not on task, leaving the room without a pass, talking back, not paying attention.

"The first time I decided not to intimidate a kid into doing what I wanted and instead asked him what he was doing, he actually *told* me. I've been doing this for a long time. You'd think I'd be able to predict what they're going to say. But I can't. It's always a new story. I don't give up. I ask questions until they've identified the choice they made and come up with a plan to handle it differently next time. This is logical but it's not natural. It takes practice. Some kids are harder bucking broncos than others, but it's worked amazingly well for me."

It also worked well for students. David created a program at Chaska High School called peer planning. When students have "low-level" behavior issues, they can choose detention or talk to a student trained as a peer planner.

"Kids have conflicts all the time, with their friends, in the halls, with bullies, with teachers, with their parents. The peer planners ask questions that help students to solve their own problems, recognize what's going on, and develop a plan," David says. "I trained about 70 kids a year, and about half of the teachers at Chaska used it, which gave us 500 peer planning conversations a year."

Choose Your Attitude = awareness

One day, as David and his class were discussing Choose Your Attitude, a student admitted he was unhappy every day at school. "I hate this place," he said. "My attitude doesn't turn around until I go to work at 4 o'clock."

"Wow," a girl said, "That must make for a long day!"

The boy didn't believe he had any control over his choice, David says, and neither do many teenagers. "They think someone or something chooses their attitude for them. They say, 'If *they* weren't doin' what *they* were doin', I wouldn't have the attitude I have.'

"...you put on your attitude like you put on your clothes."

"We talk about the fact that when you get up in the morning you put on your attitude like you put on your clothes. You're always choosing an attitude. It might be nasty, bad, or cranky. But is that the attitude you want? If not, how can you choose one that works for you?

"That's a struggle for a lot of kids," David admits, "because they don't always have another attitude to choose from. The adults in their lives haven't modeled it for them. If you have just one pair of clothes, it's hard to choose another pair."

To work through this, David's class analyzes what actually happens when an undesirable situation occurs: How do they typically respond? What does the response look like? What are some other ways they might look at the situation?

"Teenagers, like the rest of us, fall into predictable patterns. In many cases, it's victim mode. Once they recognize their patterns, they start to see how often they operate on autopilot. When they realize they can actually make a more satisfying choice, it's life changing. The situation may be the same as before; the only difference is how they choose to view it. Suddenly they feel a sense of control over their lives they never knew they had."

Likewise, when teachers consciously choose their attitudes, it can change everything around them. "I had a foreign exchange student from France named Pierre," David shares. "I like to use humor so I was doing this French accent. All of a sudden this other student blurts out, 'You say this social contract applies to all of us?' 'Right,' I said. To which she replied,

'Well, I think you're being inappropriate.'

"Now, this student did not always bring the most positive attitude to class; she was sometimes rude to other students, defiant, negative. I thought to myself, 'And you're telling me *I'm* inappropriate?' But I kept my mouth shut. She said, 'I think you are being disrespectful to Pierre.'

"I felt terrible! I said, 'If you are offended, I am sorry. I'll never do accents again. I will find another way to use humor.' She was surprised. She looked like someone had hit her with a frying pan.

"After class, Pierre came up to me in the hall. He said, 'I wanted to tell you I was never offended by your dialect. It's funny—though you are doing it all wrong. But I would like you to keep doing it, because you're the only teacher who acts like I exist.'

"I went home and thought about it, but I decided to stop using the accent. It's like sexual harassment—the rule is if you feel you're being harassed, you are. The solution is to stop the behavior. So I stopped, and it was tough. It felt like I was being watched. Other students would say to me, 'She's wrong.' And I'd say, 'If it didn't work for her, we have to honor that.'

"After a week, this girl came up to me after class. I'm thinking, 'Now what did I do?' But she says, 'I'm so sorry. I wasn't really offended. I didn't know if Pierre was offended; in fact, two days ago, he told me he wasn't. I just never thought you'd listen to me. I'm struggling in school. You honored me by listening to me, and now it's killing me.'

"She was a senior, and on the last day of school, she stopped by my office. She had two roses. She said, 'I'm giving a rose to my alternative school teacher who saved my life. I'd like you to have the other one.'

"I didn't want to do it at the time, but I made the choice to take her at her word. In the end, she made the choice to be honest with me. It was a safe place where we could do that. My job is to accept everyone who walks through my door and try to help them," David concludes. "I drove home that night knowing that I was doing the work God wanted me to do."

Make Their Day = recognition

To emphasize another FISH! philosophy, David often asks teachers to consider this scenario: At your funeral, 40 people stand up and tell how much they appreciated you, the things you did for them, and what they liked about you. Would you rather that happen after you're dead or on a day-to-day basis during your life?

"Having people talk nice about you at your funeral is great but it's like winning the lottery the day after you die; it's too late. The problem is that we aren't trained to make other people's day. We think it has to be something grand or we have to say just the right thing. But it can be as simple as a smile or a compliment."

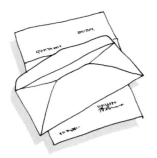

"I asked each student to compose a letter to a teacher."

As a writing assignment, David asked each student to compose a letter to a teacher who has lived one of the four FISH! principles for them. Then he asked the teachers to come to his classroom. They didn't know what was going to happen, and when they received the letter and a FISH! award, their reactions were often emotional.

"A few teachers told me they decided not to open the letter until their prep period because they knew they were going to cry. But I think the students who wrote the letters were happier than the teachers. See, a lot of kids and adults are really into themselves. FISH! is all about other people. Surprisingly, when it's all about other people, you end up getting it back for you."

David continued the activity by asking students to talk about someone else who had been there for them. A girl told about the aunt who was more like her mother. "I love her so much," she said. A homesick exchange student, missing her friends, broke down when talking about the Valentine's Day card her friend had made for her. A boy who sat in class every day, hood covering his face, rarely speaking, lit up when he recalled how good it felt to give a toy to his little brother.

"Things really changed in class after that day," David says. "People felt safe talking about things that mattered to them—family, friends, and relationships. They trusted each other."

"It's pretty cool to be that open in class," a student said later. "You don't get that very often in high school. Usually people are building walls, instead of tearing them down."

Practice, practice, practice

David says changing habits doesn't happen overnight—though that's what a lot of teachers want to do. "They go to a workshop or they read something, get inspired—which is where it has to start—but they want to change everything. Then they come in Monday morning, some kid swears, and they're off to the races doing the same thing they did before.

"I tell teachers you can't learn to swim while sitting in your classroom reading a book about how your arms flail in the water while you are parallel to the surface. The only way to learn is to dive in and start doing it.

"And," he clarifies, "it's okay to make mistakes. Teachers trying to ask more, instead of telling, would say to me, 'I tried that with a kid this morning. It worked really well for about 10 minutes, but then it all went to heck.' I'd say, 'What about those 10 minutes?' They'd say, 'It felt really good.'

"So you go home, analyze what you did, make adjustments then try again. When you get thrown off the horse, you say to yourself, 'This is too important. I'm getting back on.'"

While outside support is important, and while David feels it's helpful if FISH! is "sanctioned" by the principal or another leader in the building, he says the easiest way to kill it is to mandate it. "Forced play doesn't work. My approach, along with my wife Sally's, was to say, 'Here are some ideas that have worked for us. Take what you want.'"

With that approach, David estimates about 30 percent of the teachers at Chaska High School bought into it. "That's typical," he says.

"The easiest way to kill it is to mandate it."

"They're people who are doing these kinds of things already. FISH! affirms them. Then what happens is the over-the-fence syndrome. People say, 'It looks like you're having fun in your class. What are you doing in there?' 'Oh, we're doing FISH!' 'Really! That video we watched?' Then you start to share ideas.

"Of course FISH! will look different in a communications class than a math class. Some teachers introduce the idea of FISH!, don't do activities, but live it and model it. And it works. Others show the video and do activities to cement FISH! every week, and every time a kid chooses his attitude or makes someone's day, you make that a teachable moment.

"But," he cautions, "some teachers show the video, then do nothing with it. I think that's *worse* than doing nothing. I'd rather do nothing than put it up front and say 'Yeah, we're living The FISH! Philosophy.' The FISH! Philosophy is not an event. It's a *process*."

"The basketball coach used FISH! and won a state championship."

To help those who were interested, David and Sally created activities to help teachers and students practice FISH! (a number of which are now part of the FISH! For Schools materials) and shared them with the staff. Several young teachers, from math to English to technology, made FISH! part of their weekly curriculum. The basketball coach used FISH! with his basketball team and won a state championship (though it also helped that he had an all-state center). The dance team, struggling with unity, used it to build teamwork.

David notes, "You're never going to get everyone on board with this. But all it takes is a critical mass and even the teachers who used to be curmudgeons are affected. People, even if they don't believe in it, do it by osmosis. They may not acknowledge it, but they're doing it … a rising tide lifts all boats.

"People often ask about measurable results. How many detentions, suspensions, expulsions, in-school suspensions, time-outs, parent conferences do you have? That's one measure. When kids walk around school, is it a safe place to be? Does it feel safe emotionally? Is it safe to ask a question in the classroom? FISH! won't transform an entire school immediately, but it moved our high school in that direction faster than anything we had ever tried before."

Postscript: Reaching the reluctant learner

In the fall of 2004, David retired from Chaska after 33 rewarding years of teaching. He and Sally now help educators, students, and adults build safe, non-coercive school environments through their Restorative Learning Workshops (www.restorativelearning.com).

Looking back, his memories—and moments of true inspiration—are of the struggling or reluctant learners. He says, "Half of the kids in America don't really need us. They have the ability, the motivation, the family support to learn on their own. It's the other kids, the ones hanging on that last rung, who depend on us.

"As teachers, we do our best to make it safe, to make kids feel accepted … We give love and we get love. In the end, they leave us to go out into the world because they know they can do things for themselves," David says. "And as teachers we say to ourselves, 'This is what I was meant to do.'"

Example has more followers than reason.

—*Christian Nevell Bovee*

Thanks and Acknowledgments

According to an ancient folk saying, "It takes a village to publish a book"—okay, I made that up—but it's true. Now it's time to thank the village.

I was privileged to be a conduit for the voices of the amazing, wonderful, dedicated people whose stories appear in this book, but that work would not have been possible without the contributions of my co-authors in and around ChartHouse Learning.

John Christensen has always had a vision that the joy he encountered in his first visit to the fish market could help educators connect with the same feeling in their schools and classrooms. That vision led to the creation of FISH! For Schools, as well as this book. His enthusiasm, support, and encouragement have been unwavering

And Andy Halper ... well, he is the straw that stirs FISH! For Schools. His zeal, enthusiasm, and unfettered idealism have built FISH! For Schools into an ally that is helping educators reclaim the passion that is rightfully theirs. Andy excels at jarring people's sensibilities in a way that awakens them to more sensible ways of helping children. His methods are often irreverent, but his mission is always sacred.

Andy has assembled an amazingly talented and committed education team, and it's through their transforming, relationship-building work with educators across the country that we met many of the folks featured in the book. Mega-thanks to Ann Clark, Steve Mintz, Sheila Galligan, Millie Reid, Jeff Stafford, and Chris Streiff. Ann and Chris's stories appear in the book; they felt so strongly about the power of FISH! For Schools that they joined our staff to spread its message to other educators.

Kudos are also due to the irrepressible P.J. Wester, whose boundless energy brought The FISH! Philosophy to schools back when FISH! was still considered just a "business" program. Her pioneering work truly paved the way for today's FISH! For Schools.

Steve Mintz was the coordinator of this project and there could not have been a better choice. His strong work ethic and selfless perspective helped him to balance the various visions of all those involved, and he always made decisions based on what is best for the reader. Look up the word "integrity" in the dictionary and you'll see Steve's picture.

Elissa Gjertson's fervent and perceptive editing made the manuscript better by separating what was good from what was just okay. Her efforts gave the book a structure that made it even more accessible and, like a master conductor, made sure all the crescendos were in the right place.

Jeff Jones poured (and drew) his soul into the wonderful, touching artwork that accompanies the stories. Jeff skillfully crafted simple yet moving images that drew out and enhanced the emotions of the stories. Together with graphic artist Mary Breen, he also created the book's graphic identity, deftly balancing energy with reflection.

Special thanks to John Nielson, Stephanie Hanson, and Jenny Anderson for their creativity in marketing and diligence in keeping the publishing train on time. Thanks also to Mike Schechter for his diligent legal advice and always-amusing musings on life, and to Julie McDowell for her legal and publishing knowledge and generosity of spirit.

To the entire ChartHouse Learning crew, thank you so much for the support, laughter, and kindness that you share with us—and the world—every day. Only in the atmosphere that you create through your hard work and optimism could we even attempt what we do.

We want to acknowledge several people whose immense curiosity, continual desire to learn, and deep insights have added so much to ChartHouse Learning's understanding of The FISH! Philosophy. Thanks to Stephen C. Lundin, Ph.D., the Big Tuna, who played such a vital role in framing the philosophy, and from whose enlightening imagination came the inspiring, best-selling book *FISH!* Thanks also to Harry Geist, Carr Hagerman, Robb Harriss, and Betsy Schreyer for the great insights they have contributed to ChartHouse Learning materials; these were a helpful background resource.

And to Will Schwalbe, Emily Gould, and everyone at Hyperion, our gratitude for helping bring these stories to the greatest number of people. Your commitment to this project is making a real difference in the lives of teachers and students across the land.

We have learned so much on this journey from all the educators whose paths, luckily for us, have crossed ours. Three names deserve an extra mention. David St. Germain, Sally Bulleit, and Chris Streiff shared—out of their experiences, experimentation, and reflections—important insights about education and The FISH! Philosophy that spurred us forward, to learn and grow on our own. Appropriately, Chris and David's stories bookend this volume.

Finally, to our families and to the families of all the people mentioned above: Your love is our breath, and makes what we do matter.

—*Philip Strand, November 2005*

FISH! For Schools

Welcome back to the reason you became an educator.

FISH! For Schools helps educators create richer, more effective learning cultures.

Designed for educators by educators, FISH! For Schools combines research-based, staff-development materials, innovative classroom exercises, and live learning experiences tailored to the needs of K-12 leaders, teachers, support staff, and students.

Based on The FISH! Philosophy, which is alive in organizations throughout the world, FISH! For Schools helps educators build:

• rewarding relationships
• positive classroom management
• personal responsibility and internal motivation for staff and students
• development of the "whole student" as an engaged learner
• a safe and playful learning community
• respect for diversity
• conflict resolution skills

Standing behind FISH! For Schools are the people of ChartHouse Learning—the official home of The FISH! Philosophy—all of whom are committed to providing you with ongoing solutions, products, flexibility, and creativity to support your long-term success with FISH! For Schools.

We look forward to starting a conversation about what's possible!

Call us at 866.469.2705

Build your learning community with the SCHOOLS OF FISH! Study Guide

The Schools of FISH! study guide will help you ignite powerful, personal conversations about the kind of educator you want to be, and the kind of school community you can create.

The guide is filled with thought-provoking questions about what makes real learning happen ... and what doesn't. It can be easily adapted for:

- Staff development
- Study groups
- Book clubs
- Individual reflection
- Parent groups

Download the study guide at **www.fishforschools.com/book**

Online FISH! Resources

www.fishforschools.com

Complete online resource for FISH! For Schools curriculum, local and national workshops, books, speakers, consulting services, and fun FISH! gear. Check out free downloadable samples, stories from the Teachers' Lounge, blogs, and more.

www.fishphilosophy.com

Anything you need or want to know about FISH!, this is the place. Read stories from around the world, participate in discussion forums, purchase FISH! books and gear, find out about speakers and facilitators, or contact a FISH! philosopher.

Sources

Introduction

McNeely, Clea A., James M. Nonnemaker, and Robert W. Blum. "Promoting School Connectedness; Evidence from the National Longitudinal Study of Adolescent Health." *Journal of School Health*, April 2002, vol. 72, no. 4.

Noddings, Nel. *The Challenge to Care in Schools: An Alternative Approach to Education*, Teachers College Press, 1992, p. 175.

Smith, D. "What makes teens feel connected to their schools?" *Monitor on Psychology*, July/August 2002, vol. 33, no. 7.

Be There

FISH! THOUGHT: CONTROL VS. COMMITMENT:

Barth, Roland S. "The Culture Builder." *Educational Leadership*, May 2002, pp. 6-11.

Kohn, Alfie. *Beyond Discipline: From Compliance to Community*. Merrill Education/Prentice Hall (by arrangement with the Association for Supervision and Curriculum Development), 2001, pp. 60–61, 63.

McCaslin, M. and T. L. Good. "Compliant cognition: The misalliance of management and instructional goals in current school reform." *Educational Researcher*, vol. 21, no. 3, 1992, p. 12.

Rogers, Carl. "Beyond the Watershed: And Where Now?" *A Way of Being*, Boston: Houghton Mifflin, 1995, pp. 292-315.

Wessler, Stephen L. "Sticks and Stones." *Educational Leadership*, December 2000/January 2001, vol. 58, no. 54, pp. 28-33.

Play
"IT'S MY JOB TO CARE"

A number of quotes from Kristin Puntenney came not only from our interview with her, but also a wonderful paper Kristin wrote in 2004 called "The FISH! Experience," as part of her work toward her M.Ed. degree in secondary education from the University of Cincinnati.

Make Their Day
FISH! THOUGHT: FEAR GETS AN F

Kohn, Alfie. *Beyond Discipline: From Compliance to Community*, Merrill Education/Prentice Hall (by arrangement with the Association for Supervision and Curriculum Development), 2001, p. 103.

Spycher, Pamela. "Sticks and Stones: Teaching the Power of Empathy to Young Children." *Classroom Leadership* newsletter, December 1999/January 2000, vol. 3, no. 4, p. 7.

FISH! THOUGHT: FIRST, LIVE IT

Rogers, Carl. "Beyond the Watershed: And Where Now?" *A Way of Being*, Boston: Houghton Mifflin, 1995, pp. 292-315.

Choose Your Attitude
FISH! THOUGHT: NEW DAY, NEW CHOICES

Lundin, Ph.D., Stephen C., Harry Paul, and John Christensen. *FISH! A Remarkable Way to Boost Morale and Improve Results*, Hyperion, New York, 2000, p. 51.

FISH! THOUGHT: THE REAL SELF-ESTEEM

Reasoner, Robert. "The True Meaning of Self-Esteem." National Association for Self-Esteem website (www.self-esteem-nase.org/whatisselfesteem).

Background Reading

Boyd, Victoria. "The School Culture, School Context: Bridge or Barrier to Change." Southwest Educational Development Laboratory, 1992.

Checkley, Kathy. "Protecting Students from Harassment: It's the Law—and Then Some." *Curriculum Update* newsletter, Fall 1999, pp. 2-3.

Covaleskie, John F. "Power Goes to School; Teachers, Students, and Discipline." College of Education, Educational Policy Studies, University of Illinois at Urbana/Champaign, Philosophy of Education Yearbook, 1993.

Dyck, Brenda. "Looking at Your Students in the Future Tense." Voice of Experience, www.education-world.com.

Evans, Timothy D. "Encouragement: The Key to Reforming Classrooms." *Educational Leadership*, September 1996, vol. 54, no. 1, pp. 81-85.

Freiberg, Jerome H. "From Tourists to Citizens in the Classroom." *Educational Leadership*, September 1996, vol. 54, no. 1, pp. 32-36.

Kohn, Alfie. "Choices for Children: Why and How to Let Students Decide." *Phi Delta Kappan*, September 1993.

Noguera, Pedro A. "Transforming High Schools." *Educational Leadership*, May 2004.

Sawatzky, Jamie. "Making a Good Start." *Education Update* newsletter, September 1997, vol. 39, no. 6, pp. 4-5.

Willis, Scott. "Managing Today's Classroom: Finding Alternatives to Control and Compliance." *Education Update* newsletter, September 1996, vol. 38, no. 6, pp. 1, 3-7.

Zachlod, Michelle G. "Room to Grow." *Educational Leadership*, September 1996, vol. 54, no. 1, pp. 50-53.

About the Authors

Philip Strand is the Word Wizard at ChartHouse Learning. He is co-author of *FISH! Tales* and played a leading role in developing the FISH! For Schools program, including researching and writing the ultra-experiential Guided Journey. He has spent the last 45 years trying to recapture the promise he showed as a kindergartener and hopes this book is a start.

John Christensen is Chairman and Chief Creative Infuser of ChartHouse Learning. Award-winning filmmaker and co-author of all the FISH! books, John's insights and learning programs are voraciously utilized by corporations around the world ... and are now gleefully changing the face of education as we know it.

Andy Halper, ChartHouse Learning's Professor of Boredom Prevention, is the driving force behind FISH! for Schools. As the fearless leader of the Education Team, Andy creates experiential curriculum from the ultraviolet consciousness of all educators. A recovering academic, he offers an unparalleled slant through the phenomenology of engagement, for K through college, educators and students alike.

ChartHouse Learning
221 River Ridge Circle
Burnsville, MN 55337
866.469.2705

www.fishphilosophy.com
www.fishforschools.com

Make FISH! part of your life!

More than 3.5 million copies sold worldwide!

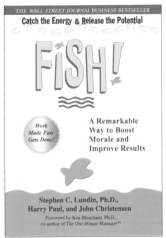

FISH!

The original book, which made a huge splash around the world, tells the story of a fictional company that transformed itself by applying lessons learned from Seattle's famous Pike Place Fish market.

0-7868-6602-0
978-0-7868-6602-1

FISH! STICKS

This brilliant business parable about keeping your company's vision alive and renewed uses the example of a fictional sushi restaurant that is always two steps ahead of the competition.

0-7868-6816-3
978-0-7868-6816-2

FISH! TALES

The insightful follow-up to the runaway national bestseller FISH! offers exciting, dramatic, real-life stories of how companies and individuals apply the "FISH! Philosophy" to boost morale and improve the quality of their businesses and lives.

0-7868-6868-6
978-0-7868-6868-1

FISH! FOR LIFE

FISH! for Life is a road map for achieving personal happiness and well-being in all areas of life by applying the FISH! principles. After all, life shouldn't be work.

1-4013-0071-5
978-1-4013-0071-5

The FISH! philosophy:

Be There ❧ Play ❧ Make Their Day ❧ Choose Your Attitude

Wherever Books Are Sold
 HYPERION   FishPhilosophy.com